summer
TIMES

summer
TIMES

A Collection of Scriptures, Meditations and Prayers

Russell J. Levenson, Jr.

Insight Press
Covington, Louisiana

Summer Times: A Collection of Scriptures, Meditations and Prayers

Insight Press, Inc.
P.O. Box 5077, Covington, LA 70434
© 2014 by Insight Press
All rights reserved. First printing 2014.
Printed in the United States of America

Cover artwork by Russell J. Levenson, Jr., oil on canvas, *Gioiosa Estate*.

Library of Congress Cataloging-in-Publication Data

Levenson, Russell J.
  Summer times : a collection of scriptures, meditations, and prayers / the Rev. Dr. Russell J. Levenson, Jr. -- 1 [edition].
    pages cm
  ISBN 978-0-914520-56-6 (pbk.)
  1. Summer--Prayers and devotions. 2. Episcopal Church--Prayers and devotions. I. Title.
BV30.L465 2014
  242--dc23
                    2014004985

Dedicated to

my wife, Laura;

my children, Evie, Jones, Luke and Jake;

my parents and all those who

through love and support made possible

countless summer memories and the lessons learned from them.

"With Special Thanks..."

I am grateful to the members of St. Martin's Church, Houston, Texas, who allowed me a sabbatical that enabled me to, along with Laura, write this little collection of devotionals. To Rebecca England, who carefully reviewed and edited the first major draft of *Summer Times*. To the Communications staff of St. Martin's, especially Maureen Vicent, who helped format the text and photos. To the Rector's staff of St. Martin's, Carol Gallion, Brittney Jacobson and Allie Hippard, who assisted with many of the final details of this work; and also Justin Jacobson who assisted with final edits. To those kind friends on the back cover who lent their support. To Dr. Fisher Humphreys and the leadership of *Insight Press,* who together adopted this project. And lastly, our continued thanks to our friends and family who prayerfully encourage and support us in our daily life and ministry together.

— Laura and Russ Levenson

CONTENTS

MEDITATIONS

Out of Place

"Be still, and know that I am God!"

— Psalm 46:10

Be still. Be still. Those two words alone seem to be a calm oasis plopped in a time of rapid-fire busyness. Our forebears, only a century ago, would not recognize our world of emails, cell phones, texts, *Skype*, Twitter and *Facebook*. Satellite radio, GPS, home audio systems, even shower televisions have made it possible to never be alone, even when you are alone. It is possible to literally fill every twenty-four hours of every day with noise, activity, work.

The ancient world in which David would pen the above words had virtually no similarities to our own. Yet even then...yes, way back then... David beckoned the human heart to *"Be still."*

This book is an invitation to *be still* and also to *consider*. *Consider* what can be learned in moments of leisure, rest—*stillness*. The former Archbishop of Canterbury, Donald Coggan, wrote, *"I go through life as a transient on his way to eternity, made in the image of God, but with that image debased, needing to be taught how to meditate, to worship, to think."*

In our multi-faceted, multi-tasking world, we tend to forget that we are actually pilgrims on a journey between two points— our beginning and our end, with another beginning at that end. In all our worked-up flurry of activity, do we take the time— the necessary time—to be still and consider? To consider who we are...in relation to ourselves, others, to our God?

"In contemporary society our Adversary," wrote Richard Foster, *"majors in three things: noise, hurry, and crowds. If he can keep us engaged in 'muchness' and 'manyness,' he will rest satisfied."*[1] Indeed, as psychiatrist Carl Jung noted, *"Hurry is not of the devil; it is the devil."*[2]

For many, the summer months are the slower ones. Of course, we can easily pack them pretty solidly as well—chores that were put off during the cold winter and rainy spring; if we are fortunate to have time off, travel; if we are blessed with children, day camps and summer sports. The

possibilities to flee from stillness are endless. But summertime whispers to us to hit the pause button.

I have entitled this little work *Summer Times*. As an Episcopalian, my spirituality is, by practice and nature, seasonal.[3] The seasons, whether they be the traditional four offered by Mother Nature, or the liturgical seasons offered by Mother Church, give us a chance to change gears. What follows are forty devotional pieces that are born out of the call to be still.

This work is not intended to be complex or heady. It is intentionally put together to be a companion at morning coffee, afternoon tea or wine, or before the lights go out with a nightcap or cup of cocoa. Portions may brush on deeper issues of our faith and its theology, but I have written more in-depth about those in my previous works. This work, instead, is simply to invite you toward that stillness that, in a particular way, reveals not only the nature of God, but our own nature and God's calling to us.

---

1   Richard Foster, *Celebration of Discipline: The Path to Spiritual Growth* (San Francisco: Harper and Row, 1978), 15.
2   Morton T. Kelsey, *The Other Side of Silence: A Guide to Christian Meditation* (New York: Paulist Press, 1976), 83.
3   My first book, *Provoking Thoughts*, was a Lenten devotional. My second, *Preparing Room*, was an Advent devotional.

In the mid-1800s, one of the most notable voices of the Christian faith was George MacDonald. In one sermon, he preached to his congregation,

> *"You know many of you are so busy, and you are not able to think two things at once, and so suddenly you come to be aware that you have been forgetting God, and that life has not been in you, and that you have been wandering this way and that way, trying to make money or doing your duty in the world... But then, when you wake up, did it ever occur to you, or does it occur to you, that it is He that is calling you?...*
>
> *"Oh, make yourselves glad with this thought, that when you have been forgetting Him, and have thought of Him, it is He that is calling you, 'Come unto Me and have life.' So we have just to lift up our hearts to Him for more life, and brace ourselves to the thing He tells us to do, whatever it be, even the duty that has been making us forget Him—we have to do it with Him instead of without Him."[4]*

I hope that your summer months are, in fact, slower than all the others, and that you can carry this companion along to help you probe into deeper, more meaningful, more restful adventures; and, as MacDonald suggests, put the work you do when you are not at rest in its proper place—at God's disposal.

I have been fortunate to have had many extraordinary and, for lack of a better word, simple but poignant experiences in my five-plus decades of life—many of them are connected to moments "away" from regular day-to-day life. Most of the experiences are peppered by shared memories with friends, family, my wife and children.

My grandmother, whom we called "Grantzy," was a spirited adventurer. She lived in the country; we lived in the city—and she always wanted to make sure we knew there was more to life than afternoon television and weekend shopping malls. It was not uncommon at all for us to be driving along in her little VW station wagon and for her to pull off the road. When she did, her grandchildren always knew we were about to experience something completely different than our day-to-day lives...something, frankly, completely new.

---

4   George MacDonald, *Getting to Know Jesus* (New York: Ballantine Books, 1980), 29-30.

She felt free to walk up to the door of a stranger who might have owned a chicken farm so that her grands could "take a tour." We did that several times, and each time we did, we always left with a gift…a small chick for each kid. One with which we would play, and even cuddle at night, during those grandmother visits; ones that would eventually end up in the growing menagerie in her backyard, and, of course, at times, on her dinner table!

Because summer is longer than forty days, I invite you not to hurry—to "pull off the road." Perhaps you will read one devotional every few days, perhaps more than one a day. However you choose to read, do so without hurrying, at your leisure, in your own time. *Summer Times* is divided into four parts. The first includes meditations inspired by the early stories in Genesis; the second by the Psalms; the third by the Gospels, and the fourth by the Epistles, sometimes called the Psalms of the New Testament. Each meditation includes a brief piece of Scripture, an initial reflection question, the core meditation, another more probing question or thought, and a closing prayer.

I offer this work as a gift, and I do so with the help of my wife, Laura, who has carefully helped me edit and review these meditations, and has offered both an introduction and authored a few of them as well. It will become obvious, quickly, that we sometimes, with gratitude, borrow the thoughts and stories of others; when possible we have

offered the appropriate citations. I also offer my thanks for life experiences that have allowed me a broader view of a world I otherwise would not have known.

I also do this knowing, humbly, that not everyone has the privilege of slower times, vacation days, or resources that allow for travel. I realize, all too well, in the words of a wonderful prayer that there are many who *"work while others sleep."*[5]

---

5   "The Service of Compline," in *The Book of Common Prayer* (New York: The Church Hymnal Corporation, 1979), 134.

However, being still does not have to involve anything more than finding a little bit of heaven wherever you are; maybe through a prayer said in the midst of five o'clock traffic, a deep breath before a busy day, an afternoon nap, a happy memory, a song that slips through your lips.

C. S. Lewis noted that these kinds of activities seem out of place in our day-to-day lives because, well, they really are. We do not always dance and play, eat and make merry; but when we do, it brings us authentic joy; when we do, we indeed are getting snapshots of heaven indeed. As he puts it:

> *"It is thus in our 'hours off,' only in our moments of permitted festivity, that we get glimpses of heaven—dance and laughter, play and momentary ecstasy—which seem frivolous, so temporary, perhaps even unimportant down here, for 'down here' is not their natural place. Here, they are but a moment's rest from the life we were placed here to live. But in this world everything is upside down...that which, if it could be prolonged here would be a truancy, is likest that which in a better country is the End of Ends...joy is the serious business of Heaven!"[6]*

So, then, let us begin, especially to consider those bits of heaven that are more clearly revealed in our hours off—our moments of rest from the life we were placed here to live. Turn the page, and let us get started. But not too quickly...slowly...deliberately...take a deep breath...be still first...then begin.

The Rev. Dr. Russell J. Levenson, Jr.
Rector, St. Martin's Church
Houston, Texas

---

[6]   C. S. Lewis, *The Joyful Christian* (New York: Scribner, 1996), 227–228.

An Invitation

by Laura Levenson

"O taste and see that the Lord is good..."

— Psalm 34:8

Russ and I would like to offer an invitation as you begin your journey with *Summer Times*. As we have wrestled together with the words that follow, a recurring theme came to mind, that of *invitation*. We realize, like anyone who attempts to write for others, that some of what we offer may hit the spot, and some may be way off the mark, depending on the reader, his or her disposition, even the time of day. We offer what we offer simply as a gift.

The biggest reminder to me that summer is upon us is the arrival of flowers, fruit, and vegetables. For many long months these plants lay dormant, storing up the water and nutrients they somehow know that they need, becoming stronger and larger until that magnificent moment when their blossoms burst forth, transforming our world into a colorful, fragrant, delicious delight.

Who has not been on wild blackberry picking expeditions down long country lanes, walking to the sound of cicadas and the smell of mown hay, searching for the green spindly plants, always set amid poison ivy, covered with red and black berries? My cousins and I spent many hours in this way in Primm Springs, Tennessee. I remember the way our hands and legs would be covered with scratches from the thorns, but we didn't feel them, we were too busy eating berries and thinking about the cobbler our Aunt Jane would make from them. Purple hands, purple tongues, betrayed us to our mothers and aunts as we returned from our search. The punishment? Hand-churning the ice cream maker, turning the handle until it would turn no more, tasting the salty water running out of the churn, checking the dash for the cream's delicious readiness, hoping the Aunts would say "It's ready!"

God designed for us a beautiful world, and every season has its own special identity. He desires to see us enjoy and use His gifts. Don't  you love watching a child or grandchild open a gift you have given to them, and delight in the look on their face as they see the new treasure? It is so much more fun than receiving a gift ourselves! God is a loving parent who put us here on earth to not only nurture and care for this place, but to love and enjoy it as well.

As you begin your journey with this little collection of meditations, we invite you simply to ask God to speak, perhaps not even where we intended as we wrote these words. Look for the blessings, the warnings, the encouragements, and please receive them as intended—as a gift; which we offer with the hope that God will perfect our imperfect offering to your benefit and the benefit of His kingdom.

Summer Time

The prayer offered in David's words from Psalm 34 is an invitation to receive gifts and enjoy them! As summer begins, remember God will smile as He sees you enjoying His lovely gifts to you. As God delights to give, will you delight in receiving?

A Prayer

Dear Lord,
We are forever thankful for the world you have given us to care for and enjoy.
We pledge to honor your beautiful works and to love them.
Thank you for the ways in which you show your love for all of us.
We praise your holy Name! Amen.

Idling

"In the beginning... God..."

— Genesis 1:1

Who or what is God to you?

Atheism, unbelief in God, is really rather uncommon in our day. There is wide belief in God, lived out in innumerable religious faiths. Within the Judeo-Christian tradition, there are literally thousands of denominations in the United States alone. There are perhaps some who honestly hold absolutely no faith in God, or "a" god, whatsoever. But I do find that to be the rare exception, not the norm. Evidence that humans have believed in a divine being since our earliest days on planet earth is on the rise, not the decline. Recent archeological findings reveal Neanderthal burial sites that clearly show that at the time of death, there was care and attention paid to the deceased. Burial sites included floral arrangements and careful placement of the body in a fetal position, leaving little doubt that, even way back then and there, even perhaps among those most simplest of minds, a "faith" existed in some thing, and likely some One, beyond the grave.

One of the prevailing concerns from the beginning of our faith was not just that we believe in God, and be in relationship with Him, but also that we put nothing else before God—that there is one God in actuality, but also that there should be only

1

one God for all humankind. Only God was to sit on God's throne.

The first of the great Ten Commandments is crystal clear that *"you shall have no other gods before me."*[1] Putting something other than God in God's place is called idolatry. The problem with idolatry is that when God is not God, we begin to lose touch with Him, His reason for creating us, and our reason for being.

Be still for just a moment or two and ask yourself if there are any competing "gods" in your life. It could be something as simple as your hobby or your work. Maybe it is a habit or a particular relationship other than God. Many people in our day have made their children an idol. Parents and grandparents hang all kind of baggage around the necks of their offspring—putting pressure on them to achieve success in a particular vocation; to marry or befriend the right people; to sign on for the right branch of the military or get into the right university; to pledge the right fraternity or sorority and so on. Can you imagine the pressure this puts on young ones? And of course, it really is not about their success; it is about idolatry.

Sometimes we think when we are sitting in traffic, when our engine is just idling, that it is a waste of time. Is it, though? Living in Houston, Texas, I spend a lot of time in traffic. I have begun, more and more, to turn off the radio. When I see a traffic jam up ahead, I usually take a deep breath and try and  relax before the crunch. When the car starts idling, I take some time to think, to pray, to look around. I usually begin to see things I have never before noticed. A new store on a familiar corner; a restaurant that has been there for years that I have never tried; perhaps a friend walking by who may need a ride or may even be in distress.

Just the other day, I saw a poor young girl on the side of the road holding a sign, "Single mom, out of work, please help." Tears were running down her face. I do not always notice, but I did this time. Fortunately, I had some spare food and the number of an agency printed out in

---

1   Exodus 20:3.

my back seat, which I keep for precisely these kinds of situations. I hopped out of my car and handed both to her. She thanked me. I got back in my car, prayed, and thought about her the rest of the day. I would not have seen her if I were not idling. Sometimes we miss a lot of things by not running on idle.

Idling is not always a bad thing; in fact, it usually is not. Sit still for the next few moments. While idling, think and ponder your possible idols. Think on the reality that idol worship separates you from God. Augustine once penned to God Almighty, *"Thus does the world forget You, its Creator, and fall in love with what You have created instead of with You."* It's sad when we do that, don't you think?

Better to idle a bit, consider the idols, and turn back to the Creator of all things, the Creator of you...for in the beginning, God; nothing else, just God.

 Summer Time

Who or what is god to you? If it is God, give thanks! If you find someone or something competing for the title, consider what you can do to rid your life of idolatry so you can fall more in love with the One who created you, rather than the things He has created.

A Prayer

Let me rest easy, dear Lord
Sitting idly by,
Let me rest easy, dear Lord
Opening my heart's eye,
Let me rest easy, dear Lord
Learning to worship You alone,
Let me rest easy, dear Lord
Receiving You, my eternal home.
Amen[2]

---

2   Prayers without a citation are written by the author.

You Look
Just Like Your Daddy

"Then God said, 'Let us make [adam] in our image, according to our likeness...' So God created [adam] in his image, in the image of God he created him; male and female he created them."

— Genesis 1:26-27

In whose image are you?

In some families, genes are very strong. Even when I was a boy, it was not unusual for a friend of one of my parent's to say, *"You know, you look just like your daddy."* I was, and still am, a big fan of my father, so I took it as a real compliment. As I grew older, I came across photos of my grandfather in his young adult years, and lo and behold, I looked even more like his image!

"Kids...let's go." When I was a young man, I learned a great deal from my father. He ran a large retail business, and my sisters and I were often sidekicks. We lived in the suburbs, and, unlike some of my friends, did not have lake or mountain homes. Because of my

father's full work schedule, it was hard to get away to go camping or fishing, so he would purposely make time to spend with us. This time usually began with the words, *"Kids...let's go;"* and off we went to the bowling alley, the movies, to play putt-putt. I suppose it was not just genes that made me "look like my daddy," but the time I spent with him during these mini-vacations.

The old, old story tells us that humankind, male and female, was fashioned in the image of God. It would be a bit overly simplistic to believe that God has arms, legs, hair, eyes, and ears as we do. The Bible also tells us that God is "spirit," meaning, by nature God is probably not physical in the way you and I know physical.[1] However, we, you and I, are still created to look "just like our daddy" or "just like our mommy."

Spend some time with this question, "In whose image are you?" I purposely do not end that phrase with the word, "made," because frankly many in today's world have forgotten or lost touch with the reality that we are all created in God's image, and instead have tried to fashion themselves in an image of their own making. My mentor John Claypool used to tell me, *"One of the real problems with our human nature is that while we may believe we are created in the image of God, we too often try to return the favor."*

If the person in the mirror looks more like a person of your own making, and not like the image of God, then something certainly is awry. Spending some time with this question about image may reveal to us that we are allowing ourselves to be made in the image of something we were not intended to be. Maybe I want to be made in the image of a great humanitarian—such as Albert Schweitzer or Archbishop Desmond Tutu; perhaps a well known capitalist like Warren Buffet or Bill Gates; maybe a historic hero such as Abraham Lincoln or Rosa Parks; or a well-known celebrity, politician, athlete, and so on. It may just be the guy down the street or the woman who works across the hall; but you were not...**you are not** created in

---

1   John 4:24.

5

those images. You were created in the image of God Almighty.

When you lose touch with that, even for a moment, you lose touch to some degree not only with God, but also with your reason for being. One of the best ways to go back to that image, again and again, is to respond to His simple words, *"Kids...let's go."* To rest your image not in anyone's hands but His by spending more and more time with Him...at work, at play, at rest...when all is silent...when loudness shatters the quiet, just be with God. In time, you know, you will look in the mirror and hear a divine whisper, *"You look just like your daddy."* Toward that end, image *is* everything.

 Summer Time

In whose image are you? Are you made in God's image? Or are you being made in an image of your own making? What can you do, concretely do, to put yourself in His presence more and more? What can you do to get in touch with the reality that you are, indeed, made in His image?

A Prayer

Almighty God,
by Whose spoken Word
all things came into being,
speak yet again within me
that by Your Holy Spirit
I may increasingly become
the child you created me to be
in Your image, Your very own.
Amen.

Fruit Stands

"God blessed them, and God said to them, 'Be fruitful and multiply, and fill the earth and subdue it..."

— Genesis 1:28a

Do you relish God's creation?

Most of our summer vacations were spent on the Gulf beaches of south Alabama and northwest Florida. Before high speed expressways were built, these trips often took an entire day as we drove slowly through one small town after another. Peppering the edges of every single one of these towns were wonderful fruit stands.

While we did not stop at all of them, we usually stopped at many and "stocked up" for the beach week ahead. The larger ones were under tents, cooled not by air conditioners, but by large space fans, blowing flies away and causing the tents to flap in response to their oscillations. Tables stood like rectangle cornucopias pouring out before us an ocean of colors, smells, and tastes—okra, peppers, eggplant, vine ripe tomatoes, apples, sweet potatoes, peaches, dark green watermelons and dimpled cantaloupes. We would load up our bags, carry along the tasty gifts, and usually get started on a juicy peach before the car pulled away from the stand.

When God created man and woman, He told them the fruit of every plant was theirs to consume, use, and be nourished by; and He reminded them that they were gifts, *"I have given you every plant yielding seed that is upon the face of all the earth, and every tree with seed in its fruit; you shall have them for food. And to every beast of the earth, and to every bird of the air, and to everything that creeps on the earth, everything that has the breath of life, I have given every green plant for food."*[1]

When someone gives us a gift it is usually an expression of their love for us. But it is given with the hope that we will enjoy it...relish it. God gave, and gives, lots of things for lots of reasons. Some of those reasons are deep, mysterious, and serious; some however are simply for the pleasure of His children—rich food and drink, time with loved ones, a good night's rest. God gives because He loves. And as He loves, His gift comes with the hope that it will bring us joy.

Mirroring the stoics of old, some skewed interpretations of our faith would suggest life is not to be so much enjoyed as endured. Clearly that was not God's intent when He birthed creation, and it is not His intention now.

My hunch is that somewhere today, God will put a fruit stand before you. It may be an invitation for a cup of coffee with a workmate, or an unexpected call from an old friend. It may be the fish you did not expect to catch or the joke that brought a smile to your face. You know, it is okay to enjoy it. It is okay to really relish God's

---

1   Genesis 1:29-30.

8

creation. Enjoying life is a byproduct, if you will, of stopping at God's fruit stand. As Paul Tillich suggested, *"Joy is the emotional expression of the courageous yes to one's being."* Why not take some time today to enjoy what fruits God brings your way, not because you should, or because you have to, but because in receiving and enjoying you bring great delight to your Heavenly Parent?

 Summer Time

Consider what fruit stands God Himself may place before you this day. Can you receive them as gifts? Can you enjoy them? Can you relish them and, as you do, give thanks as well?

A Prayer

In the beginning, God made the world:
>   Made it and mothered it;
>   Shaped it and fathered it;
>   filled it with seeds and signs of fertility;
>   filled it with life and with endless ability.
All that is green, blue, deep and growing,
>   God's is the hand that created you.
All that is tender, firm, fragrant and curious,
>   God's is the hand that created you.
All that crawls, flies, swims, walks or is motionless,
>   God's is the hand that created you.
All that speaks, sings, laughs, cries or keeps silence,
>   God's is the hand that created you.
All that suffers, stumbles, lacks or longs for an end,
>   God's is the hand that created you.
The world belongs to God.
The earth and all its people.
>   — From *The Iona Community*

He Did, You Should

"Thus the heavens and the earth were finished, and all their multitude. And on the seventh day God finished the work that he had done, and he rested on the seventh day from all the work that he had done. So God blessed the seventh day and hallowed it, because on it God rested from all the work that he had done in creation."

— Genesis 2:1-3

When do you rest?

Henry David Thoreau penned these stark words about work without rest, *"The laboring man hasn't leisure for true integrity daily. No time for anything but to be a machine."* Wow...a machine. Tough words, but true to the bone.

When God finished His work of creation, we are told *"He rested."* We live in a world that prizes hard work—no quarrel with that, but we also live in a world where authentic rest is sometimes seen as laziness. There is, of course, such a thing as laziness and the Bible was not too keen on that vice.[1] But rest from hard labor is something God did; and it was so important that His children followed His lead. Rest was woven into

---

1   See for instance Proverbs 10:4, 12:27; Ecclesiastes 10:18; Titus 1:12; Hebrews 6:12.

the Ten Commandments, *"Six days you shall labor and do all your work. But the seventh day is a sabbath to the LORD your God; you shall not do any work..."*[2]

Without physical rest, the body literally begins to break down; health gives way to exhaustion and illness. But without spiritual rest, time set aside for God, our soul begins to give way to spiritual sickness. Rest is an absolute necessity in one's spiritual health. God rested, and if the Creator of the universe did it, so should we.

The question for your consideration today is *"When do you rest?"*[3] I know some people who go on vacation and then, well, do not really rest. They carry along all the electronic gadgets that keep them distracted from everything and everyone around them. I also know people who habitually use their off-day simply to catch up on household chores. No doubt some of these are necessary realities in the workaday world, but they should not be at the expense of resting.

A life without rest tends to conceal what is really going on—a discomfort with silence and solitude, reinforcing an illusion that we are the masters of our own souls. On the other hand, voluntary rest can restore our confidence in God by reconnecting us to Him. Richard Foster reminds us *"If we are silent, who will take control? God will take control."*[4] That is not a bad thing, is it?

Are you following God's lead? Are you obeying His command?

---

2   Exodus 20:9–10.
3   Not "How do you rest?" We will get to that too!
4   Foster, *Celebration of Discipline*, 101.

Summer Time

Not all of us are blessed to able to rest a full day in seven; and some of us work much more than a typical eight-hour day, but that does not negate God's model, nor His command. When do you rest?

A Prayer

My spirit longs for thee
Within my troubled breast,
Though I unworthy be
Of so divine a guest.

Of so divine a guest
Unworthy though I be,
Yet has my heart no rest
Unless it come from thee.
Amen.

— John Byrom, d.1763

Watch Your Step

*"The LORD God commanded the man, 'You may
freely eat of every tree of the garden; but of the
tree of the knowledge of good and evil you shall
not eat.'"*

— Genesis 2:16-17

....

Are you using your freedom wisely?

I spent most of the summer prior to my freshman year in college
studying at a Sea Lab along the Alabama Gulf Coast. While much of our
work was in the classroom and lab, there was also a great deal of work in
the field; and the field for budding marine biologists is the sea. On a few
occasions, we used our small vessel for less noble causes than collecting
specimens, and instead caught our dinner by dropping a large drag net.

Our maritime grocery cart would be hoisted out of the water, bulging
with some of the finest shrimp the Gulf had to offer. A pull of binding
and the entire contents would spill out all over the deck. Students were
then free to choose their own, but sifted in the rich harvest were some

dangerous foes—crabs
with sharp pincers,
stingrays whipping
barbed tails to and fro,
the poisonous lionfish
and stinging man-of-
war. A careless move,
choosing poorly, even
a careless step could
mean a nasty wound,
or worse, a trip to the
hospital. Everything

13

that fell on the deck was there for the taking, but not everything was good for the takers.

However you wish to interpret what was going on between God and the first humans in the Garden of Eden, it is clear that part of God's plan was to give humans freedom to choose—freedom to choose right and

freedom to choose wrong. It is also clear that there were far more opportunities to choose right than there were to choose wrong. Our divinely-created forebears could eat of all the trees they wanted, but they were warned to stay away from just one.

For the most part, you and I are free to choose—our friends, our spouses, our habits; what we eat, drink and how we use our free time. Virtually all of these "freedom of choice" opportunities include both right and wrong offerings. We never regret making the right choice; we almost always regret making the wrong ones. St. Frances de Sales wrote, *"We have freedom to do good or evil; yet to make choice of evil, is not to use, but to abuse our freedom."*

God's gift of freedom tells us a lot about God's parental policy. God is a loving God, not a controlling God. As loving parents counsel, coach, and guide, but do not *"control"* their child; God sets before us a myriad of opportunities, tells us where to go, but leaves the freedom to choose up to us. As the church father Origen suggested, *"The power of choosing good and evil is within the reach of all."* Hmmm...watch your step.

Summer Time

Are you using your gift of freedom wisely? In the myriad of choices before you, right now, have you identified the choice you should not make? How will you live into that decision?

A Prayer

Give us, O Lord, a steadfast heart,
     which no unworthy affection may drag downwards;
give us an unconquered heart,
     which no tribulation can wear out;
give us an upright heart,
     which no unworthy purpose may tempt aside.
Bestow upon us also, O Lord our God,
     understanding to know you,
     diligence to seek you,
     wisdom to find you
     and a faithfulness that may finally embrace you;
through Jesus Christ our Lord.
— Thomas Aquinas, d. 1274

The Gift of Shame

"And the man and his wife were both naked, and were not ashamed."

— Genesis 2:25

....

Where do you hunger for righteousness?

We have all seen it; at the beach, or lake, or perhaps the public pool—a young toddler strips down to his or her bare essentials and struts with all the pride of a peacock with its train of feathers in full flare, not a care in the world, not a lick of shame. When I see this, frankly, I get a bit nostalgic, perhaps even a bit jealous. Living over half a century, I have plenty in my life about which I am ashamed. When I see a shame-less child, there is a part of me that wishes I could go back to that season of innocence.

We are told that God's original intent was for His children to live without shame; to have a footloose and carefree lightness to life that is not burdened by the companions of guilt and regret. Shame was introduced when the wrong choice was made, and it became the gift that kept on giving right down to our very day. But is that really a bad thing?

Without shame, we would not know when we have stepped out of line. Without guilt we would not know when we have hurt ourselves, or our loved ones. Without regret, we would trample all over the gift of life with our perpetual tendency (also known as original sin) to fall, stumble and sin.

Mark Twain once quipped, *"Man is the only animal that blushes. Or needs to!"* The only problem with Twain's words is that men and women are not animals. They are beings created in the image of God. When we feel that divine *"blush"* come over us, it may very well be revealing that we have stripped ourselves bare in a way that we should not have. Toward

16

that end, the gift of shame invites us toward one of Jesus' most beautiful of promises, *"Blessed are those who hunger and thirst for righteousness, for they will be filled."*[1]

So when you see that young one toddling away, perhaps diaper in hand, and you get that internal nudge just to go back to a day without shame, take it not so much as condemnation, but as a road sign, pointing you to the One who can fill you when you are hungry to do the right thing.

 Summer Time

Where, in your life, do you hunger for righteousness? In what ways are you feeding that hunger? Will you let God do that for you?

A Prayer

O good Jesu, word of the Father, the brightness of the Father's glory, Whom angels desire to behold; teach us to do Your will; that guided by Your good Spirit, we may come to that blessed city where there is everlasting day and all are of one spirit; where there is certain security and secure eternity and eternal tranquility and quiet felicity and happy sweetness and sweet pleasantness; where You, with the Father and the Holy Spirit, are alive and reign, one God for ever and ever. Amen.

— St. Gregory, Bishop of Sicily, d. 628

---

1   Matthew 5:6.

Truth Hiding

*"Then the eyes of both were opened, and they
knew that they were naked; and they sewed
fig leaves together and made loincloths for
themselves. They heard the sound of the LORD
God walking in the garden at the time of the
evening breeze, and the man and his wife hid
themselves from the presence of the LORD God
among the trees of the garden. But the LORD God
called to the man, and said to him, 'Where are
you?' He said, 'I heard the sound of you in the
garden, and I was afraid, because I was naked;
and I hid myself.' He said, 'Who told you that
you were naked? Have you eaten from the tree of
which I commanded you not to eat?'"*

— Genesis 3:7-11

Is it time to 'fess up?

Almost everything about it was wrong. I had trained as a scuba diver, and had several practice dives in various freshwater springs. But this was my first open water dive with three of my fraternity brothers. We took a small boat (wrong) three miles out into the Gulf (wrong). While people knew we were going, no one really knew exactly where (wrong). We rented equipment we did not thoroughly check out (wrong). We did not take a dive master with us (wrong). We split up in pairs (wrong). When my friend and I descended 60 feet to the bottom we could not find a place to secure the anchor so we left that to our comrades (wrong).

18

So now, working in reverse order—my equipment went on the blink and began free-flowing air from my respirator. I was running out of air quickly, more quickly than I thought. We began to swim back to where the anchor "was" (gone by the way). As we followed the track it left in the sand I took my last breath before the air went completely out. My friend and I began to buddy-breathe to the top. When we did pop up, our boat was nowhere to be seen (no anchor—means free-floating boat). We were floating three miles out, land was a distant sight, no air in the tanks, and no signs of help.

The fact that I am telling this story means we did make it back (much longer story). I remember when we were pulled into the boat, I flopped on the deck, let out a big sigh and said, *"Let's just go back home."* I suppose I could have blamed a lot of people for that pickle I was in, but really, the only one to blame was little old me.

In the Garden, God laid out the rules. *"Here is a gift...use it...enjoy it...go here...don't go there...as long as you do that, you'll love it here...you'll have no shame...cross the line and all kinds of bad things will begin to happen."* Of course, we know how it turned out. Tempted to *"be like God,"* the first humans ignored the very first and essential divine directive, and, literally, all hell broke loose.[1] What we are told is that as soon as humans began to disobey, they reaped what they sowed. Bad choices bear spoiled fruit, no way around it.

While the gift of shame may nudge us towards innocence, at times, we have a tendency to sidestep the truth and blame our wrong choices, our sins, on others. As soon as God began to question Adam, he pointed to Eve; Eve pointed to the snake, and so on. As soon as they did it, they knew what they did was wrong, and rather than 'fess up to God, they sought to hide both literally (covering themselves) and verbally (evading God's cross-examination).

The best way to deal with an infection is to spot it, name it, and then find the right antibiotic to treat the sickness. The best way to deal with our sins is to name them. We must come to terms with the truth that our actions, thoughts, and feelings may be a source of pain and brokenness in our relationship with God, with others, and even ourselves.

Adam and Eve got caught with proverbial hand-in-cookie-jar disease, followed closely by foot-in-mouth disease. How much better it would have been just to come clean! Eventually they did, of course, and when they did, they had to pay the price of consequences for their actions. But they did not lose relationship with or the love of their God.[2]

Poet Jonathan Swift wrote, *"Never be ashamed to own you have been in the wrong; it's but saying you are wiser today than you were yesterday."* As the old saying goes, confession is good for the soul. Indeed.

 Summer Time

Take some time; consider where you may be hiding the truth. What might you need to 'fess up to begin a fresh start? Covering it will just mean the burden of guilt will grow. Exposing it, however, allows for the healing to begin. Augustine wrote, *"Before God can deliver us we must undeceive ourselves."* Why not begin today?

---

1   Genesis 3:5.
2   Read on, Genesis 3:12–24. Adam and Eve's relationship with God was forever changed, and they were given burdens to bear, including being expelled from Eden, but they were still children of God created in His image.

A PRAYER

Jesus said, There is joy among the angels of God
Over one sinner who repents.
Come to me all who labour and are heavy laden
And I will give you rest.
God has promised forgiveness to all who truly repent,
Turn to Christ in faith, and are themselves forgiving.
In silence we call to mind our sins.

Silence
Let us confess our sins.
Merciful God,
We have sinned
In what we have thought and said,
In the wrong we have done
And in the good we have not done.
We have sinned in ignorance;
We have sinned in weakness:
We have sinned through our own deliberate fault.
We are truly sorry.
We repent and turn to you.
Forgive us, for our Saviour Christ's sake,
And renew our lives to the glory of Your name. Amen.

A Pronouncement of Forgiveness
Through the cross of Christ God have mercy on you,
Pardon you and set you free.
Know that you are forgiven and be at peace.
God strengthen you in all goodness
And keep you in life eternal. Amen.

— From A New Zealand Prayer Book,
He Karakia Mihinare o Aotearoa[3]

---

3   Michael Counsell, comp. *2000 Years of Prayer* (Harrisburg: Morehouse, 1999), 503.

Divine Layover

> *"He brought him outside and said, 'Look toward heaven and count the stars, if you are able to count them.' Then he said to him, 'So shall your descendants be.'"*

> — Genesis 15:5

Are you willing to wait?

It was the longest layover I had ever experienced in flying. For a season, I traveled several parts of the Orient, and on a flight from Tokyo to Hong Kong, we stopped in Taipei, Taiwan. Once we landed, we were told that our ultimate journey would be delayed for an undetermined amount of time. I had been waiting a long time to travel to Hong Kong. Though my friends and I knew we would ultimately get there, the wait, perhaps over half a day, was at times unbearable.

Layovers are a common part of travel; in fact waiting is part of making almost any journey. Since we have yet to invent viable transporters (a la *Star Trek*) nor can we travel at lightspeed (a la *Star Wars*) our journeys, whether from your house to a friend's, from one state to another, or from one continent to another, begin and end with some form of waiting.

There is a lot of waiting in the stories of Scripture...a lot...there is almost always a huge span of time between a promise God makes and the fulfillment of that promise. Whether it is Moses delivering the Hebrews

22

to the Promised Land, Mary delivering the Lord of Life, or Jesus putting up with the endless squabbles of His own disciples, it just seems to be part of God's *modus operandi* to expect His followers to learn to live with the gift of waiting.

Before God renamed him, Abraham went by the name Abram. Abram and God were tight, as we might say today. They were very close; they talked, it seems, as you or I might talk to a good friend or a family member. For a long season, Abram carried a heavy heart that he may not have children. He was sad that should he die, not his blood kin, but a servant in his household would inherit his possessions.

In the midst of all of his fretting, God had Abram go outside, look up into the heavens and look at the stars. *"Take a look,"* God said, *"Don't worry...your offspring will be as numerous as the stars in the sky!"*

In the next meditation, we will take a look at what God might have really meant with that promise, but for now, let's agree that it was a promise worth holding on to for good old Abram. In the story that follows, we do see that there was a long wait, a kind of divine layover, between this promise and its fulfillment. Sometimes Abram waited patiently on the Lord, and other times he did not. He lost faith; he tried to control the circumstances so that the promise of the Lord came to be not on God's terms, but his own.[1]

It is hard to wait sometimes. Our world is one of instant gratification in virtually every form, but our ways are not God's ways, and clearly the antibiotic to our frustration with God's divine layovers is patience. Evelyn Underhill reminds us, *"Patience with ourselves is duty for Christians and the only humility. For it means patience with a growing creature who God has taken in hand and whose completion He will effect in His own time and way."*

Such patience, however, requires trust—trust that what God has promised, or what you have prayed for, will in time be met with an end of God's making. If it is God's end, then whether your layover is longer than you thought or takes you to places you did not expect, it is still the right end of the journey.

---

1   When Abram's wife, Sarai, did not become pregnant within Abram's timetable, Abram chose, at Sarai's suggestion, to sleep with a maidservant from his household named Hagar. Hagar did become pregnant with a child, but the trouble that arose out of the conception, and ultimately, the birth, of Ishmael was a heavy burden in Abram's household.

If you entrust your hopes and your journey to God, is not the end something for which the wait is worth enduring?

We did eventually make it to Hong Kong. Once we got there, it was more exciting than I could have imagined. It was worth the wait, the diversion, the layover. Perhaps that is often, if not always, true of waiting!

 Summer Time

Consider something for which you are waiting. A relationship to heal? A work situation to improve? Word from an old friend? News from the doctor? Why not give way to the waiting not as an intrusion, but as an opportunity to trust even more the One who is our perfect end?

A PRAYER

O God of peace,
Who hast taught us that in returning and rest we shall be saved,
in quietness and in confidence shall be our strength:
By the might of Thy Spirit lift us,
we pray Thee,
to Thy presence,
where we may be still and know that Thou art God;
through Jesus Christ our Lord. Amen.[2]

---

2   *The Book of Common Prayer*, 832.

The Birthplace of Righteousness

"[Abram] believed the LORD; and the LORD
reckoned it to him as righteousness."

— Genesis 15:6

What inspires you to do the right thing?

Like many of you readers, during my grade school years I attended my share of summer camps. One camp was just south of my home in Birmingham, Alabama. I remember it as an idyllic place where I learned to hike, fish for bream on a cane pole, and water ski. I knew family friends had something to do with the camp, but not until adulthood did I connect the dots that the camp was really a large family property that they generously shared as a day camp and as a gathering place for a wide variety of charitable and church-related functions.

Over the years, our family became close to these generous camp owners. One day, without our inquiry, our request, and at no cost to us, they offered it as a timely and much-needed getaway for my wife, kids, and me. The respite began with a short list of instructions, the keys, and a wish to simply have a good time. We always did, and made our own memories there. The gift itself gave us a sense of gratitude and birthed in us a desire to always care for the place as if it were our own.

What is the birthplace of doing the right thing? What really drives us to what the Bible calls "righteousness?" If your area of the country is in any way like mine, there are a number of television preachers—most of whom seem to believe that our behavior is not the fruit of relationship, but of fear. We act as good people not so much because we "want to," but because "we have to," or...well...else.

In the last meditation, I said that I would touch on what God's promise of numberless children meant to Abram. Abram, whom God eventually renamed Abraham, did become father to a few children, but he became the spiritual father of children without number—children that exceeded the number of stars in the sky, believing children who, like Abraham "believed." Abraham is actually seen as the patriarch of the three great world religions—Judaism, Christianity and Islam. In the Christian faith, however, we see Abraham as the prototype not just for how we understand righteousness, but also for how we live it—how it becomes more than a just a word.

It is good that we get this word "faith," not tucked in some obscure, hard-to-find verse in Scripture, but in the first book—setting the stage for a recurring theological theme that is echoed again and again.[1] Put simply, the pathway to right living is right relationship. Because we know (or should know) that God loves us, we are filled with a desire to live in good, right, loving ways. *"We love because he first loved us."*[2]

The problem with focusing on "right behavior" rather than "right relationship"—is that we all fail the "right behavior" test. When we focus solely on right actions, then we become riddled with guilt, shame, and a sense of failure. Pastor Charles Swindoll writes about this, suggesting:

---

1   See Habakkuk 2:4; Romans 1:17; Galatians 3:11; Ephesians 2:8–9.
2   I John 4:19.

By living like that, we develop a worst-case mentality. That is like my taking my keys and handing them over to one of my teenagers who just got a drivers license and saying, "Now let me remind you, you're going to have a wreck. So the first thing you need to do is memorize the phone number of our car insurance agent. That way, when you have an accident you can be sure to call the right number. But here are the keys. Hope you enjoy the drive."[3]

When God took Abram out under that night sky, He made a promise to our ancient patriarch. We are told the promise came not because Abram deserved it, or earned it, or had never stumbled or fallen, but because God willed it...it was God's gift, God's decision to bless Abram. In response, Abram's belief and trust in his relationship with God is what God deemed righteous.

What makes a marriage? The vows or the love between husband and wife? What makes a friendship? Being the perfect friend or having affection for one another? What inspires loyalty in sports or military service? The jersey? The uniform? Isn't having a right relationship the birthplace of living the right way?

Not too very long ago, my family and I once again were given the gift of that lake home. My son and I hiked and fished, and he learned to ski in the very waters where I had learned so many years ago. When our time was over—we cleaned up, washed the linens, took out the trash—not because we had to, but because we wanted to, in response to a wonderful gift born of mutual affection... born of love.

---

3   Charles Swindoll, *The Grace Awakening* (Nashville: Thomas Nelson, 1996), 124.

Summer Time

What inspires you to do the right thing? Is it fear? Guilt? An attempt to somehow make up for wrong things? To balance the scales? When it comes to God, would you rather be "right" or be in a "right relationship"? If you know that "Abram believed and God credited that to him as righteousness," how does that change your understanding of righteousness? If you know that "we love because He first loved us," how does that change your motivation to do the right thing?

A PRAYER

Behold, Lord, an empty vessel that needs to be filled. My Lord, fill it. I am weak in the faith; strengthen me. I am cold in love, warm me and make me fervent that my love may go out to my neighbor. I do not have a strong and firm faith; at times I doubt and am unable to trust You altogether. O Lord, help me. Strengthen my faith and trust in You. In You I have sealed the treasures of all I have. I am poor; You are rich and came to be merciful to the poor. I am a sinner; You are upright. With me there is an abundance of sin, in You is the fullness of righteousness. Therefore I will remain with You, of whom I can receive but to whom I may not give. Amen.

— Martin Luther, d. 1546[4]

---

4   Mary Batchelor, comp. *The Doubleday Prayer Collection* (New York: Doubleday, 1997), 59.

Sometimes It Takes Two...

"Is anything too wonderful for the LORD?"

— Genesis 18:14a

What is our Lord calling you to do?

In the early 1980s, long before it was one of the hottest vacation spots in Mexico, my wife and I chose Cancun as our honeymoon destination. One day, one of us had the bright idea that we would take a bicycle built for two, also known as a tandem bike, on what we thought would be a short journey on the outskirts of town to some unearthed Mayan ruins known as *Las Ruinas del Rey* (The Ruins of the King). Outskirts, we found, ended up being several miles from our hotel. We considered abandoning the idea several times—especially as the road got rough, after we took a wrong turn or two, and the sun began to beat down. But of course, there's one thing about a tandem bike—it takes two to make the trip!

The little verse from Genesis is nestled into a much larger story.[1] In the last few meditations, we have been considering God's relationship with Abraham, which was, in part, focused on his desire to have a child. In this scene, the promise is now about to be realized as three angels visit Abraham and tell him that even in their old age, the ancient patriarch and his wife, Sarah, will soon conceive a child.

This is not the first, or last time, we see God and humans working together. God, of course, can work on His own, but He chooses to work in tandem with His children. Think of Noah building the Ark, Moses and the Hebrews crossing the Red Sea, David standing up to Goliath, Mary conceiving the child Jesus, Peter and John before the Sanhedrin, and so on. God could have worked any of these great

---

1   If you have the time, read Genesis 18:1–15.

biblical sagas without a partner, but He chose instead to work not as One alone, but as two.

What a bold thing to think upon...a humbling thing...to come to believe that for a reason of God's own choosing, you have been singled out to do a work of God's own design. It may be something beyond your imagination, or it may be as simple as picking up the phone to call a lonely neighbor. Whatever it is, if God is inviting you to a divine partnership, it is significant in His eyes.

My new bride and I did make it to those Mayan ruins, and in doing so we forged a memory that will last a lifetime. It took both of us working together to get there, and to get back. It was of little importance to anyone else, but of great importance to the two of us. When you get down to it; there are a lot of things we cannot do on our own; sometimes we need someone along for the ride, and perhaps that other needs us as well.

The same seems to be true of a God who often works alone, but who also allows for the truth that *sometimes it takes two*. As Abraham learned, sometimes we need a partner. Nothing is too hard for God to accomplish. And when He is our partner, the sky's the limit.

Summer Time

What thing may God be calling you to do today? Notice there is a difference between something you want to do and something God may be calling you to do. Think on that a bit...pray on it...what, if anything, is stopping you?

A Prayer

God of all good things,
Quiet the voices competing for Yours alone;
Still the wanderings of my mind,
My heart,
My soul,
And in that silent place You create,
Let me receive Your invitation, and
With a mingling of my humility and Your boldness,
Ever walk and serve
Within Your perfect will.
Amen.

Which Way to Go

*"Happy are those who do not follow the advice of
the wicked, or take the path that sinners tread."*

— Psalm 1:1a

....

Are you on the right path?

As I wrote earlier, for many years I was an avid scuba diver, (I did
get much better after my "out of air" incident!). When each of my
children turned sixteen, I gave them scuba lessons and each time, I
reenrolled and went back through the classes with them. I also joined
them on their first open water dives. Most of those dives were rather
easy, shallow, and fun; but a few were more dangerous, even risky.

One such dive was into a deep water spring in central Florida. Though
our little group was made up of experienced divers, and though we
had a dive master along, we were asked to circle up so that we could
clearly learn the risks involved with this particular dive. It was deep,
nearly 100 feet. At about 50 feet, it would require that we push
our way through a strong current coming out of the spring into an
underwater cave. Once in the cave, we could descend the next 50 or
so, but there was a point beyond which we were not to go. We were
shown a map of the dive; we were given clear guidelines. We were
given the opportunity to withdraw our participation. My son and
I did not, and because we followed the instructions, the dive itself
ended up being safe and memorable.

This is the first of two meditations on Psalm 1. Though the author
and date of its writing are unknown, the psalm sets a fairly clear stage
as to which way to go. In this part, we are told that the man or woman
who steers clear of dangerous places is blessed. That seems pretty
simple, but as you and I both know, we do not always go where we
should. In the same way our dive instructor mapped telling us where

we could and could not safely go, this psalm holds up a spiritual map, making it clear that steering clear of the path of the wicked is the avenue toward a blessed life.

Earlier, I wrote that the Judeo-Christian faith teaches that the birthplace of righteousness is a "right relationship" with our Lord. But having that right relationship does not give us a free pass to live as we want. There are things we can do, paths we can walk, that damage that relationship and in some cases, even break it. Our Lord never stops loving us, but our Lord does not turn a blind eye toward wickedness. Of those who live outside the boundaries of the safety net of Psalm 1, we are told they, *"are like chaff that the wind drives away. Therefore the wicked will not stand in the judgment, nor sinners in the congregation of the righteous."*[1]

No question about it, we all draw outside the lines at times. There is only One who walked the earth who could include the word "perfect" in His resume. But how marvelous that God holds up maps so we know which way to go. When we make a wrong turn, the map is still there to get us back on the right road. When it comes to this kind of righteousness—won't you dive in?

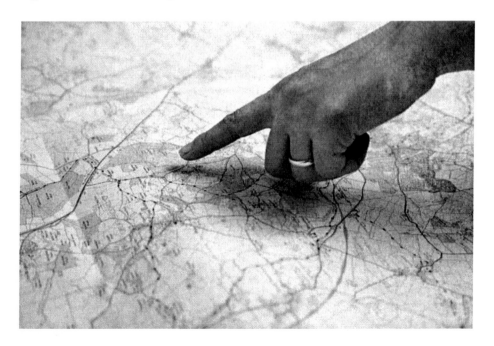

---

1   Psalm 1:4–5.

Summer Time

Read through all of Psalm 1. Where does it speak directly to you today? To a specific area of your life? Your relationships? Your habits or work? Are you on the right path? Can you let this roadmap help guide you to a more blessed life?

A PRAYER

Lord, you have given us Your word as a light to shine on our path. Inspire us to meditate on that word, and follow its teaching, that we may find in it the light which shines more and more until it is perfect day; through Jesus Christ our Lord. Amen.

— Jerome, d. 420[2]

---

2   Counsell, *2,000 Years of Prayer*, 30.

Delighting in Rules

"Happy are those
> *who do not follow the advice of the wicked,*
> *or take the path that sinners tread,*
> *or sit in the seat of scoffers;*
but their delight is in the law of the Lord,
> *and on his law they meditate day and night.*
They are like trees
> *planted by streams of water,*
> *which yield their fruit in its season,*
and their leaves do not wither.
In all that they do, they prosper.

The wicked are not so,
> *but are like chaff that the wind drives away.*
Therefore the wicked will not stand in the judgment,
> *nor sinners in the congregation of the righteous;*
for the Lord watches over the way of the righteous,
> *but the way of the wicked will perish."*

— Psalm 1

Can you delight in the rules?

As I noted in the last meditation, this is the second reflection on the roadmap Psalm 1 puts before us. In this portion, we are told that unlike the wicked, the righteous actually "delight" in the law of the Lord. Delight? In the Law?

I suppose anytime I leave my home for a journey—a simple walk down the street, drive to a friend's house, a camping trip, or cruise, there are always certain things I need to do to enjoy the journey. For instance,

looking both ways before I cross the street protects me from danger, as do "Stop" and "Yield" signs. It is important to take along enough water for the hike or to pay careful attention where to gather, to "muster," should the ominous announcement to abandon ship be made!

I do not know about you, but I tend to get bothered when I notice rule breakers—someone who brings their dog on a beach where dogs are not allowed, the parent who lets his or her child in the workout room without supervision, or the woman who breaks in line at the amusement park. These "rule breakers" can get me riled up! But when it comes to my observation of the law, I am not always so quick to rile. There are times when deep down somewhere I think some rules apply, but not always, and certainly not to me!

Then again, we are told for the man or woman who finds delight in the law of our Lord, we grow like trees planted right by streams of water. What a wonderful promise. In God's house there are house rules. The more we allow ourselves to be ruled by those rules, the more fruitful our lives will be.

Consider a practical example from marriage. In my marriage vows, I promise to love, honor, and cherish. Because I am not without selfish motives, I frankly do not always live into these vows as I should, and sometimes I even fail to keep them. This does not nullify the value of the vows. When I do not live into them, my marriage suffers; when I do, my marriage is nourished and grows deeper and richer. My *delight* in the rules of marriage brings me a marriage in which I *delight* as well.

There is also a freeing aspect to this understanding of keeping the rules. We keep the rules not so much because the "or else" is hanging over us like the sword of Damocles. We keep the law because we love what the law brings to us—security, a sense of meaning and purpose, joy, and perhaps above all, peace—with ourselves, with God, with others.

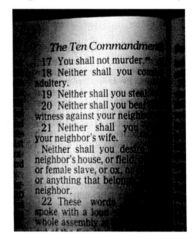

No one lived by the rules more than Jesus Himself. He did not question or balk at God's way, because Jesus knew that was the best way. As John Claypool wrote, *"Jesus was able to say, 'Thy will be done,' ...because He had come to believe that from the very beginning God's will for Him was utterly good and could be trusted."*[1]

I suppose not all the rules we humans devise are noble and life-giving. But of this we can be sure; God's rules—God's Laws—are there to point us toward greater life and peace. They bring to us a life in which we can surely delight. Perhaps we should return the favor?

 ### *Summer Time*

Think on some of the laws of our faith. Perhaps start with the Ten Commandments (Exodus 20:1–17). Move on to the Beatitudes of Jesus (Matthew 5:1–12). In reading through these, do any of them make you wince just a bit? If so, why? In what ways do these bring life to you? Where they do, can you take delight?

A Prayer

Lord Jesus,
Give me, I pray, a heart that desires to follow You...
    to follow Your Way;
    the Way of Truth and light and life.
Give me courage to face where I am in the wrong,
    where I have broken Your laws of goodness and love;
Give me contrition that I may mourn my own sin;
    so I can be restored, free, and washed anew.
And as You give Your Law that I may love You more,
    that I may love all you send my way;
Give me also, I pray, a love for that Law,
    a love born not of fear, but of delight,
That you love me enough to show me the path to
    Your perfect peace. Amen.

---

1   John Claypool, *The Light Within You: Looking at Life Through New Eyes* (Waco: Word Books, 1983), 212.

Crying, Laying, Waiting

"Give ear to my words, O Lord;
give heed to my sighing.
Listen to the sound of my cry,
my King and my God,
for to you I pray.
O Lord, in the morning you hear my voice;
in the morning I plead my case to you,
and watch."

— Psalm 5:1-3

....

What do you need or want to lay before our Lord this day?

It was late and a friend and I had rather foolishly caught a subway train into downtown Tokyo. It was our first night in Japan and we were so excited to see the city that we found our way in, but quickly realized we could not find our way back home.

If you know the Japanese culture, you also know that they take very seriously hospitality toward others, even strangers. Fortunately, we found someone who not only could tell we were lost, but also quickly came to our aid. In no time at all our cry for help was heard and we were on our way back to our temporary home.

The psalm above is David's earnest cry for help. Though David, a king, no doubt had many things at his disposal, there were times that his own power was not enough. When he was literally at his wit's end, he would cry out to God. We see these kinds of prayers throughout the Psalms. In this case, David feels beset by enemies and he seeks desperately to be delivered and guided to a place of rescue.

Be honest now. If you were to cry out to God right now for some deep need, what would it be? Something as simple as more money in the bank? More time with loved ones? A moment's peace? Perhaps something more desperate—a broken relationship restored, a child who has run off the rails, a job situation that seems hopeless, an undiagnosed illness?

David is bold, is he not? *"Give ear...give heed...listen..."* These are almost spoken as commands! But of course, we know they are the utterings of one who has nowhere else to turn. What keeps us from coming to God with those desperate cries? Maybe deep down we feel God cannot be fully trusted. Perhaps we believe we can handle it better on our own. But when deep need hits a brick wall, David shows us to whom we should take it—without reservation, without doubt.

In fact, David shows us that we should take such need to God with certainty, waiting in expectation for God's meeting of that need.

I like how Richard Foster counsels us on this point of bringing our needs to God;

> *"Jesus taught us to pray for daily bread. Have you ever noticed that children ask for lunch in utter confidence that it will be provided. They have no need to stash away today's sandwiches for fear none will be available tomorrow. As far as they are concerned, there is an endless supply of sandwiches. Children do not find it difficult or complicated to talk to their parents, nor do they feel embarrassed to bring the simplest need to their attention. Neither should we hesitate to bring the simplest request to the Father."[1]*

I am so thankful my friend and I ran into that kind fellow late at night in a strange country. I am grateful he seemed to almost know our need before we laid it before him. As we did, and waited for his guidance, sure enough, he delivered.

How much more will God meet your deepest need. Bring it to Him now.

 ## Summer Time

No need to hold back now—lay it before God. Make a list if you need to do so; cry if so inclined; whisper if so moved; yell if you think it makes the point. Then, as David did, wait...just wait...and see how God will meet your deep need with His gracious hospitality.

---

1   Foster, *Celebration of Discipline*, 40–41.

A Prayer

O God,
Early in the morning I cry unto you.
Help me to pray
And to think only of you.
I cannot pray alone.
In me there is darkness
But with you there is light.
I am lonely but you leave me not.
I am feeble in heart but you leave me not.
I am restless but with you there is peace.
In me there is bitterness, but with you there is patience;
Your ways are past understanding, but
You know the way for me.
O heavenly Father,
I praise and thank you
For the peace of the night.
I praise and thank you for this new day.
I praise and thank you for all your goodness
and faithfulness throughout my life.
You have granted me many blessings:
Now let me accept tribulation from your hand.
You will not lay on me more than I can bear.
You make all things work together for good
For your children.

— Dietrich Bonhoeffer, d. 1945
Written in 1943 for his fellow prisoners[2]

2   Batchelor, *The Doubleday Prayer Collection*, 286-287.

A Refugium for Your Troubles

"The Lord is a stronghold for the oppressed,
 a stronghold in times of trouble.
And those who know your name will put their
  trust in you,
  for you, O LORD, have not forsaken
  those who seek You."

— Psalm 9:9-10

Where do you turn for refuge?

One of the ways you and I take breaks from everyday life, particularly if we do not have the resources to hop on a plane or time to take a long car journey, is to develop a hobby—to have a skill that brings us not only a sense of personal satisfaction, but also a momentary "escape." While most of the things we do in life, even if we enjoy them, are mandatory (think of work, eating, sleeping, and so on) hobbies are actually things we choose to do, a way in which we actually give away some of our valuable time and energy, and often our tangible, financial resources. Golf, tennis, needlepoint, coin collecting, hunting, fishing—for most of us, these are not vocations, these are vacations!

I am blessed to have a wide variety of interests and hobbies, and one of those, for virtually all of my life has been keeping aquariums—outdoor koi ponds as well as indoor freshwater and saltwater reef tanks. Each present their own challenges, but perhaps those most unique have been the saltwater tanks. It is possible to build an ecosystem of fish, invertebrates and coral right in your own living room. Sometimes my tanks have required something called a refugium. It is not, obviously,

a common word, but it shares the same root as the word "refuge." Both come from the French word, *refugié*, a noun that literally means to "take shelter or protect."

In a saltwater tank, the refugium is usually out of sight—hidden from view. It is a separate tank that feeds into the larger tank, bringing nourishing oxygen, a balance of ph and sometimes serving as a food supply for the various creatures living in the seen world. The refugium literally serves as a life-line for such tanks, protecting the various life forms from harmful and life-threatening diseases.

David's psalm recalls for the reader that the ultimate life-support system, that the ideal refuge is God, and God alone. All of us are beset by angst, anxiety, and "times of trouble" like David, but behind the seen world of troubles rests the unseen God of refuge and safety.

Too often, we humans have a tendency to turn to temporary ultimately dissatisfactory places for refuge. The most common that come to mind are addictive substances, money, wealth, and perhaps fame; but of course none of these provide the kind of eternal refuge that we find in the stronghold of God.

A long tradition among churches is the practice of painting the main exterior doors of the church a bright red. In more brutal times than our own, a red door meant safety for one who might be fleeing from invading enemies or even government authorities. The red door meant safety and protection to the fearful and troubled and, for the most part, was respected by those in pursuit. The one seeking refuge knew, without a doubt, that once through the doors, they could be at peace.

In today's world, when you and I are looking for refuge, not every door is a safe door, not each one stepped through brings protection. Permanent security rests only in the divine refugium you and I know as God. As George MacDonald once suggested, when one commits his or her life and hopes to Christ, the one committing should remember God's special protection and *"ought to be afraid of nothing."*

Afraid of nothing! Wow. What a wonderful hope for those looking for a refugium for their troubles. That is certainly a hobby worth your investment.

 Summer Time

When troubled or anxious, where do you turn for solace? The apostle Peter reminded the Christians of the early Church to "Cast all your anxiety on Him because He cares for you," (1 Peter 5:7). Is Jesus your "red door," or not? If not, then how can you more fully turn away from all those other doors? If so, give thanks and walk on through!

A Prayer

My dearest Lord,
Be Thou a bright flame before me,
Be Thou a guiding star above me,
Be Thou a smooth path beneath me.
Be Thou a kindly shepherd behind me.
Today and evermore.
Amen.

— St. Columba, d. 597

Healing the Hidden

"But who can detect their errors?
Clear me from hidden faults.
Keep back your servant also from the insolent;
do not let them have dominion over me.
Then I shall be blameless,
and innocent of great transgression.
Let the words of my mouth and the meditation of my heart
be acceptable to you,
O LORD, my rock and my redeemer."

— Psalm 19:12-14

....

Where do you take your hidden faults?

I spent many days and nights in various summer camp venues, a few times lasting close to a month.

One afternoon I was horsing around with some of my friends, running through the cabin we shared, when the ball of my foot ran directly into a well positioned shard of wood sticking out of the floor. I remember

it hurting abominably. A counselor took the quick route of pulling it out with pliers; it measured about an inch and was fairly thick around. I was relieved, but unbeknownst to me, he had left a pretty good sliver still lodged deep in my foot.

45

It was not until I stepped on it in just a particular way some weeks later that pain shot up through my foot and into my leg. The unveiling revealed a large infection. The nursing care was fairly Spartan at this camp, and so handing me a tongue depressor to bite on to relieve the pain, the one and only trained health care professional was finally able to dig out the remaining foreign object, which paved the way for a complete healing.

You know, no one saw that little piece of wood deep in my foot; it was even hidden from me! But left untended, an infection grew and would have only become worse were it not tended to by the right person.

Psalm 19 is interesting to say the least. It begins by declaring the glory of God in creation, and ends with a plea for forgiveness of hidden faults and protection from willful sins. Most students of the Bible know that David was no stranger to hidden sins. As a willful participant in adultery and murder, David was likely haunted with guilt much of his life.[1] However, he still turned to the only One who could really heal.

It is human nature to try and hide those things of which we are embarrassed or for which we feel guilty. From Genesis to Watergate, "cover up" has been a fairly consistent mode of dealing with hidden faults. But neglected faults become infections.

There is a story, whether it be fact or fiction, about the painting of Leonardo da Vinci's *The Last Supper*. Leonardo was known to use models for his various works of art and after a long search, found a young nineteen-year-old to depict Jesus in the painting. For six months, he worked painstakingly on this leading character of the painting, but he would work six years more trying to find the right models to stand in for the various apostles.

When it came time to paint the betrayer of Jesus, Judas Iscariot, da Vinci once again set out on a quest for just the right face—someone with a hard and calloused face, marked by the kind of greed and sin that would enable him to betray the Lord of Lords. His search finally led him to a dungeon in Rome where he met a man who had been sentenced to die for the crime of murder. The man had long, unkempt hair and his countenance portrayed someone long acquainted with evil and despair.

After receiving the permission he needed, the prisoner was taken to Milan and was allowed to sit for the painting. When da Vinci finished,

---

1   See II Samuel 10–12.

he turned to the guards and said, "I have finished, you may take the prisoner away." But the prisoner broke loose and rushed up to da Vinci with the words, "Do you not know who I am?" Leonardo studied the man's face for a long time, and then said, simply, "No, I have never seen you before you were brought to me out of that dungeon in Rome." The prisoner lifted his eyes toward heaven and said, "O God, have I fallen so low?"

He then said, "Look at me again da Vinci, for I am the same man you painted just seven years ago as the figure of Christ!"[2]

This story reminds us of the effects of right and wrong when not tended by the Great Physician. One who once could stand as a model for the figure of Christ, only a season later, following a life of sin and crime, could sit in for the most notorious betrayer ever known.

Despite his hidden faults and battles with willful sins, David still knew to whom he could turn. With a plea from the heart to wipe away all sin and shame, David became innocent and even pleasing in the sight of God; who healed not just the visible sins, but the hidden as well.

2   J. John and Mark Stibbe, *A Box of Delights* (London: Monarch Books, 2001), 186-187.

Summer Time

What are you trying to hide from the One who knows all things? In what way may it be infecting you—your heart, your soul? Can you name it now? Can you join David in his plea? Are you ready to experience the true innocence that only God can give?

A PRAYER

Oh God, Oh Almighty God,
I lay my life before You;
Help me to name the darkness within me,
Those things known to You and to me alone.
Give me courage to face my own selfishness and sin.
Birth within me
A desire for innocence,
A hunger for purity,
A thirst for blamelessness.
Then, by the power of Your Holy Spirit,
Assuage my desire,
Feed my hunger,
Quench my thirst,
By forgiving me through the tender grace and mercy of Your Son,
Who is my Savior, my Rock and my Redeemer.
In His name I humbly pray.
Amen.

Forsaken, But Not Forgotten

"My God, my God, why have You forsaken me?
Why are you so far from helping me, from
the words of my groaning?
O my God, I cry by day, but you do not answer;
and by night, but find no rest."

— Psalm 22:1-2

Do you feel forsaken?

This will not be an easy meditation to read, so if you are not in the place to receive it today, let me encourage you to move onto the next meditation and return to this one later.

The summer after my first year of seminary training, I served as a chaplain at a hospital in Annapolis, Maryland. While I had some tough moments (I was assigned to the cardiac intensive care unit), for the most part my days were spent visiting with patients who were either on their way into or out of care for heart issues. There were exceptions.

One morning, as I came to work, I checked in near the emergency room. I noticed that one of the thick windows that separated the waiting room from the more triage-centered care areas was broken through with a hole the size of a human fist and several spider web-like canals running out from its center.

"What happened there?" I asked one of the nurses. "Oh, it was horrible," she said. "Late yesterday, a driver accidentally swerved his car off the road and hit a boy on his bike. It pinned him to the wall and his body was severed in two. There was nothing we could do. When we told his father he had died, he put his fist through that glass."

I did not know what to say, but I know what I felt—*God, where were you? Could You not have protected this young kid, these parents, from that horrible pain?* This was early in my ministry, and I would ask that question many more times. It was a question I asked as I sat with parents whose newborn was delivered with only part of his heart, and as they held the child all day until it finally died. I asked it when I walked into an emergency room with a father to identify the body of his son—a young man I had less than a year before married to his beautiful bride—after he was killed in a tragic construction accident. I asked it as I sat with a lovely couple who had worked hard all of their adult lives, but at retirement's beginning, the husband began a long, slow journey with lymphoma toward the end of his life, leaving behind their hopes of travel and time with grandchildren.

There are times when we feel forsaken by God, when suffering just does not seem to fit into the matrix of what you and I might believe to be the concept of a "loving God." *This meditation will not solve that dilemma for you.*

"Eli, Eli, lema sabachthani?" which, in a mix of Arabic and Hebrew, literally translated means, *"My God, my God, why have you forsaken me?"* These are the same words our Lord cried out from the Cross at the end of His earthly life.[1] Maybe Jesus was reaching back to Psalm 22, or maybe it was exactly what He felt. "God...have you forsaken me? Left me? Abandoned me?"

Many years ago, I was fortunate to spend an evening with Rabbi Harold Kushner, who wrote the now well-known book entitled *When Bad Things Happen to Good People*. During our time together, he said, "You know, if I would have written a book entitled, *'Why Bad Things Happen to Good People,'* it would have been very short...in fact it would have only been four words: 'I do not know.'" Thank goodness for the

---

1   Matthew 27:46.

good old rabbi's honesty, an honesty born of his own pain of the death of his son to progeria, a rare accelerated aging disease.

We really do not know *why* we suffer; we just know that we do. But what do we do with that suffering? My mentor, John Claypool, who experienced the pain of the death of his own ten-year-old daughter to leukemia, used to tell me "despair is presumptuous." What he meant, of course, equating suffering with nothingness was to shortchange the human saga and its relationship with God. Notice that the question *"Why have You forsaken me?"* does not deny the existence of God. The sufferer (whether it be David in Psalm 22 or Jesus from the Cross) does not cease to believe because of suffering, but only asks "Where are You in this?"

That may be the real question to ask—for the wife who sees her marriage crumbling, the father who sees his daughter running off the rails, the African-American pushed to the back of the line; or the laborer unjustly paid or fired. "Why?" That is a fair question. It is actually the question Job asked again and again. We often say "Ah, he has the patience of Job..." But if you know Job's story, you also know Job ran out of patience! He shook his fist at God and asked why he suffered. And God's answer was, simply "I am God."[2]

That does not sit well for most of us I suppose, with one exception—it tells us we may feel forsaken, but we are not forgotten. Suffering does not mean God is against us. For whatever reason, it is simply part of the human experience. Perhaps that is why God began the path of our reconciliation and redemption not with victory, but with suffering. God, who is Christ, and Christ, who is God, worked in tandem with the Spirit to make the ultimate revelation of God an image of the Suffering Servant—a God hanging on a tree. The well known

---

2   God's answer in full can be found in Job, Chapters 38–41.

19th-century preacher, Charles Haddon Spurgeon once said, *"As sure as ever God puts His children in the furnace He will be in the furnace with them."*

So let me end as I began, with a hard, though telling, story to read. As I learned much from my time with Rabbi Kushner, I also learned much from a day with Elie Wiesel, the Nobel Peace Prize winning author and concentration camp survivor. I was fortunate to have both some private and public moments with him, but was powerfully struck when he told of a particular day in Auschwitz.

In the presence of the prisoners, a young boy had been tortured and hung as a message to those imprisoned in the camp. The Nazi captors forced the prisoners to walk, one by one, and to face the young executed child in the face. Wiesel said he remembered hearing someone behind him whisper, *"Where is God? Where is God now?"* At first, he had no answer, but then he said, from deep within, he heard a voice say, *"Where is He? He is here...He is hanging on this gallows."*

This is a long meditation, longer than most in this little collection, but suffering is an important experience with which to wrestle. Just remember, when suffering comes, which it will, you may *feel* forsaken, but you are *not* forgotten, because the God of heaven did not slight earth, nor the trial of human suffering. Why? Because He loves us, and to love us He chose to be as we are, know what we know, so we could, in time, know we worship a God who does not abandon us to our suffering, but is instead with us, right in the midst of it.

As Psalm 22 begins to wind down, its author writes, *"For he did not despise or abhor the affliction of the afflicted; he did not hide his face from me, but heard when I cried to him."*[3] Hold fast to that. Hold fast. He is already holding fast to you.

---

3   Psalm 22:24.

Summer Time

Name your suffering. It may be something from today, from dozens of years ago, or something you know is waiting for you yet. Name it. If you feel forsaken, cry out—as did David, and Job and Jesus Himself. Cry out and know you have a God who never forgets you, and who does hear, and in His time, and in His way, will comfort and may even redeem your suffering.

A PRAYER

O Lord God, our heavenly Father, regard, we pray, with Thy divine pity the pains of all Thy children; and grant that the passion of our Lord and His infinite love may make fruitful for good the tribulations of the innocent, the sufferings of the sick, and the sorrows of the bereaved; through Him who suffered in our flesh and died for our sake, the same Thy Savior Jesus Christ. Amen.

— The Scottish Episcopalian Book of Common Prayer, 1929

Holding Fast to the Shepherd

"The LORD is my shepherd, I shall not want.
He makes me lie down in green pastures,
he leads me beside still waters;
he restores my soul."

— Psalm 23:1-3a

....

Who is your shepherd?

In Blount County, Alabama, tucked deep into the woods, there is a fascinating cave. It is not a tourist attraction. There are no signs that point the way to the opening, and you have to find a local to get you there. But *Bangor Cave* was one of those off-the-road spots that my grandmother took her "grands" to visit.

Before we got there, she told us that during prohibition, a small-time gangster by the name of "The Yellow Kid" had set it up as a speakeasy. Wiring the cave with electricity, he filled it with gambling tables, food service, a dance hall carved into the stone, alcohol and with all of that—customers. I was old enough to think Grantzy might have been slightly tugging on our legs but, armed with small Ray-O-Vac flashlights, we were off to explore.

When we got to the cave's entrance, it was a spooky sight for sure, but with our grandmother leading the way, we stepped beyond its opening. We did not have to go far to see that, lo and behold, she was telling the truth. The dance floor was still in place, as were cooking areas, and carved steps leading into a second large room. Our flashlights were frankly too weak to reveal much, but Grantzy pressed on through a second large room and up steps toward a third. On the way to the third, the passageway got smaller and all the kids felt not only a bit claustrophobic, but also felt "The Yellow Kid" breathing down our necks!

Grantzy had been to the cave before—several times evidently. She knew the way in, and the deeper we went, the tighter we held. When the adventure was coming to a close, she knew the way out. She knew her grandchildren well, knew how far they would and could really go, and guided us safely home.

The 23rd Psalm, sometimes called "The Shepherd's Psalm," is perhaps the best-known of all the Psalms, and perhaps the most famous of Bible passages. Even those not familiar with its words will often join in chorus when it is read at funeral services.

The relationship in the time of David between sheep and shepherd was vital. A good shepherd cared for his sheep; and sheep who trusted their shepherd knew he cared for every aspect of their well-being—food, water, rest, safety. Centuries later, Jesus would use the analogy of the shepherd/sheep relationship to describe His relationship with His followers, *"I am the good shepherd. I know my own and my own know me, just as the Father knows me and I know the Father. And I lay down my life for the sheep."*[1]

You may know that a common practice of identifying sheep to their owner is to paint a certain area of their body with a particular color of paint. The first time I ever saw this was in a field, only a few dozen yards from the ancient mystery we know as Stonehenge. Sheep were set behind makeshift gates on virtually all sides near that primitive circle of stones. I was fascinated to see that some had marks of blue, others green, some pink or red. The "mark" identified the sheep to its owner, in much the same way branding identifies cattle to their owner.

---

1   John 10:14–15; see also John 10:11–13.

Those of us who follow Jesus sometimes get a bit confused about who our true Shepherd is. We turn to the wrong things for comfort and security. The wrong shepherd would be as different for each person as each person is from the next. The point is that for Christians there should be only one Shepherd; and our identifying mark is His Cross—the symbol of the lengths to which God has gone to show His love for us, and the symbol of our pathway back to Him.

The philosopher Plato described the world of the unreal as a kind of cave out of which humans seeking real meaning, purpose, and life need to emerge. Fortunately, if we turn loose of any false shepherds and hold fast to the true and only One—our deepest wants will be met, and He will lead us to green pastures, still waters, and a restoration of our very souls. He really is the Good Shepherd.

 ### *Summer Time*

Are you holding fast to the Good Shepherd? Are there other shepherds you should release so your grip on the true One can be all the more fast? What steps can you take today to let Jesus lead you to places that and people who will truly help restore your soul?

A PRAYER

O Jesus, Good Shepherd,
Without You,
      a weak and hungry lamb am I,
      dry with thirst, parched of peace.
Too often I have fed on pastures not of Your own tending,
      and lost my way,
      wandering far from the child you have created me to be.
Bring me home, O Christ,
      Bring me home.
Silence all voices but Yours,
      bring to life within me, I pray,
      a sheep that hears its only Shepherd's voice.
Turn not just my ears, but my ways, that as I hear,
      I too will follow
      the Source of life,
      Who,
      assuages all hunger, satiates all thirst;
Who, by Your mercy, finally and fully
      meets all my wants, and not for my sake alone,
      but also for Yours,
Restores...
      restores...
         my soul.
Amen.

Seek and Hide

"Then I acknowledged my sin to you,

and I did not hide my iniquity;

I said, 'I will confess my transgressions to the Lord,'

and you forgave the guilt of my sin. Selah

"Therefore let all who are faithful

offer prayer to you;

at a time of distress, the rush of mighty waters

shall not reach them.

You are a hiding place for me;

you preserve me from trouble;

you surround me with glad cries of deliverance. Selah"

— Psalm 32:5-7

....

What are you hiding?

I would bet that at some point in your childhood, perhaps most especially in summer, you played a game of Hide and Seek. There are variations of course—*Kick the Can* was one of my favorites; though I did not much like the water version, *Marco Polo*, in large part because it involved getting water splashed in the face and up the nose!

In any case, it was good fun, and to some degree, exciting to run at the word "Go!" and to know at the end of the countdown that someone would be searching until you were found. If your hiding spot was the best, you usually won the game; if not, and you were the first to be found, you were "It," and the seeking became your task.

This portion of David's psalm is set within a larger context in which we see him grappling with his sin. Because many of David's psalms seem to deal with issues around guilt, forgiveness, and mercy, some might say he had a bit of a guilt complex; but as mentioned in an earlier meditation, he did have a good bit about which to feel guilty.

What David does for us here is remind us that it is no use trying to play hide and seek with guilt. He was probably familiar with the old passage from Numbers that served as a warning to his Hebrew forebears, *"be sure your sin will find you out."*[1] For whatever reason, David knew that hiding his sin was not good, so he sought out a hiding place of his own, one that would protect him from trouble and free him from the burden of guilt.

In this case, he says once he found his true *"hiding place,"* it would be as if songs of deliverance were ringing all around him. What a beautiful image!

A few meditations back, we considered the goodness that comes with forgiveness, but we did not really focus on the deliverance that comes along with it. Forgiveness wipes away the wrongdoing, but deliverance actually frees us from having to carry any burden of guilt whatsoever.

That kind of release is hard to swallow in our world, which seems to almost feast on the wrongdoing of others (as if we do not all have our own bag of rocks!). You may have experienced the forgiveness of another that is not really full forgiveness—a kind of forgiveness that mouths "I forgive," but always manages to find a way to hold it over your head, which, of course, is not true forgiveness. But what David reveals for us is that God's forgiveness does not come with strings attached.

Thankfully, God's game of *seek* and *hide* is really quite simple. If you *seek* Him out for forgiveness, He will grant it and *hide* your sins

---

1   Numbers 32:23.

59

not only from you, but from His own eyes, as if it never happened. Later David would write, *"as far as the east is from the west, so far he removes our transgressions from us."*[2] It is a reality of which the apostle John would later remind his Christian readers, *"If we confess our sins, he who is faithful and just will forgive us our sins and cleanse us from all unrighteousness."*[3] You see here, not just forgiveness, but a purification—a kind of nullification of the existence of what happened. That is what we call deliverance.

Do you remember the well-told story of when Abraham Lincoln was asked at the end of the Civil War how he would treat the Confederates who had now surrendered to the Union? The questioner no doubt expected Lincoln to offer a sharp rebuke and propose all kinds of humiliations and punishments. But no, Lincoln is said to have simply said, *"We're going to take them back as if they've never been away."*

God's game of hide and seek takes forgiveness to a higher level than simply an exchange of "I am sorry" and "I forgive." God's forgiveness does something human forgiveness is almost incapable of doing— forgetting. If you are seeking an ultimate hiding place for those things that haunt your conscience, let the game end in the merciful arms of God, for in those arms there is deliverance indeed.

 ## *Summer Time*

Are you ready not only to give God your sin for His forgiveness, but to also give Him your guilt for His deliverance? He wants to offer that, you know. Why not let God love you not just as forgiven sinner, but as one who has never been away? He loves you that much! Perhaps it is time to join Him in that kind of love.

---

2   Psalm 103:12.
3   I John 1:9.

A PRAYER

Have mercy on me, O God,
according to your steadfast love;
according to your abundant mercy
blot out my transgressions.
Wash me thoroughly from my iniquity
and cleanse me from my sin.
For I know my transgressions,
and my sin is ever before me.

Create in me a clean heart, O God,
and put a new and steadfast spirit within me.
Restore to me the joy of your salvation,
and sustain me in a willing spirit.

— From Psalm 51, of David

Meeting Your Desires

"Take delight in the LORD, and he will give you the desires of your heart."

— Psalm 37:4

What are your deepest desires?

Since my wife and I married, one of our annual traditions has been to travel to her Uncle Neil and Aunt Bea Jobe's for the Fourth of July weekend. Their home, nestled deep in the woods near a place called Primm Springs, Tennessee, is surrounded by acres of rolling hay fields and abundant vegetable gardens, encircled by a wide creek filled with "critters" galore. Even thinking of it, as I write, plants in me a bit of solace that is hard to describe.

The Jobe home has always been a place of abundant hospitality. The penultimate unveiling of that hospitality is the annual Fourth of July picnic. It is open to everyone in the county willing to come. There is no cost to attend, but people are invited to bring their own favorite dish to share as a supplement to the fried catfish that the Jobes provide and have been preparing since early in the morning. After a singing of the National Anthem, a patriotic speech or two, and a heartfelt prayer, the bountiful buffet is opened.

As the daylight begins to wane, tummies topped off with sweet tea and blackberry cobbler produce gentle smiles which open to quiet conversations between friends new and old, loved ones and family members. Hardly one of these special days passes without the feeling that, at least for that afternoon, every real need is met.

Psalm 37:4 has been an inspiration for humans in need since its inked Hebrew text first melted onto parchment. Read it again, *"Take delight in the LORD, and he will give you the desires of your heart."* There is an obvious caveat there; not necessarily all of your desires are promised, but the *"desires of your heart."*

If one were to list all of his or her desires (perhaps you would like to take a moment to do that now on the blank space below) it might include a hodgepodge of things—a new car or refrigerator, a raise or winning lottery ticket, perhaps a date with someone, or just a nice, uninterrupted meal with a loved one. My list might include tasty food without the side effects of cholesterol or triglycerides! But the promise of the psalm is not for any of those things; the promise is if one delights in the Lord, the desires of the heart are met.

Now what are those desires? Those deep desires may have different words, but my experience from my ministry tells me that for the most part, they are the same—peace, security, freedom, hope, love—things that really cannot be bought or obtained through the meeting of our physical desires.

63

Anne Morrow Lindbergh revealed some of her own deepest desires in a wonderful little book called *Gift from the Sea;*

> *"I want first of all—in fact, as an end to these other desires—to be at peace with myself. I want a singleness of eye, a purity of intention, a central core to my life that will enable me to carry out these obligations and activities as well as I can. I want, in fact—to borrow from the language of the saints—to live 'in grace' as much of the time as possible. I'm not using this term in a strictly theological sense. By grace I mean inner harmony, essentially spiritual, which can be translated into outward harmony. I'm seeking perhaps what Socrates asked for in the prayer from the Phaedrus when he said, 'May the outward and inward man be as one.' I would like to achieve a state of inner spiritual grace from which I could function and give as I was meant to in the eye of God."[1]*

Let me go back to that Fourth of July gathering for a moment. Remember I wrote that everyone is invited to bring their "favorite dish." But in exchange for coming to the big wonderful banquet with a favorite dish,

everyone is given so much more—and as they share, they are filled, not just with the nourishment of food, but fellowship.

God invites us to bring our "favorite dish" of desires to Him, and to trust that bringing those will, in turn, mean that we receive far more in return than we could have ever imagined. There is a catch though; the delight you seek must be released in favor of a greater delight—a delight in the Lord. Allowing that delight to be born, then, means, you receive the desires of your heart.[2]

You might remember that Jesus makes a similar promise to those who bring their many desires to God, *"strive first for the kingdom of God and*

---

1   Anne Morrow Lindbergh, *Gift from the Sea* (New York: Random House Books, 2003).
2   This will be addressed a bit more in the next meditation.

his righteousness, and all these things will be given to you as well."[3] Jesus did not promise that every single desire would be met, but the deepest desires that are the fruit of seeking God first, will, in fact, be satiated.

If you seek to live so that the inner person and outer are the same, to live in grace, a core of existence that enables both an inward and an outward harmony, then Psalm 37 has just the recipe for you—delight yourself in the Lord and He will give you the desires—*of your heart.*

 Summer Time

If you have not already done so, make a list of the desires that first come to mind. How can those be met?

Now, beside that list, write those that are your heart's desires—your deepest desires. Can you bring them to God, delight in Him and find He is all you really need?

A Prayer

We taste thee, O Thou living bread,
And long to feast upon Thee still;
We drink of Thee, the fountain-head,
And thirst our souls from Thee to fill.
Our restless spirits yearn for Thee,
Where'er our changeful lot is cast;
Glad when Thy gracious smile we see,
Blest when our faith can hold Thee fast.

— St. Bernard of Clairvaux, d. 1153

---

3   Matthew 6:33.

An Undivided Heart

"Teach me your way, O LORD, that I may walk in your truth; give me an undivided heart to revere your name."

— Psalm 86:11

What story does your mask tell?

One of the ways we spend our leisure time is by going to plays and performances. Some years ago, my wife and I took in the play based on Robert Louis Stevenson's 1886 novella entitled *The Strange Case of Dr. Jekyll and Mr. Hyde.*

There is a refrain that runs throughout the play sung by various cast members setting the theme for the rest of the play. The words are written by Frank Wildhorn and the first few verses are,

> *There's a face that we wear*
> *In the cold light of day*
> *It's society's mask,*
> *It's society's way,*
> *And the truth is*
> *That it's all a facade!*

Most of us can probably identify with the lyrics. You know the larger story Stevenson put together about a man in search of a serum that might enable humanity to squelch the bad in favor of the good—the kind of internal pendulum swing with which we all live.

Our faith teaches that a life lived for God is inspired and invoked to live without that split personality. But it also acknowledges that we will always, on some level, this side of heaven, struggle with a trifecta of challenges between who we are called to be, how we live into that, and how we do not. That does not mean, however, we give in to the struggle.

The prayer of David that is Psalm 86 offers one avenue toward bringing peace to that struggle—prayer. It is a plea for God's intervention into our own facades—a desire to have both the outward and the inward person be not just one, but also one who submits to God's teachings. Becoming "one" may reveal to us a great gift—an *"undivided heart,"* and an authentic fear of the Lord.[1]

For some, an undivided heart may seem to come easy; for others, the struggle is not so. Even the apostle Paul, it seems, wrestled with this. Writing to the Romans, he offered, *"I do not understand my own actions. For I do not do what I want, but I do the very thing I hate."*[2]

The late John Stott mirrored some of these words,

> *"Who am I? What is my 'self'? The answer is that I am a Jekyll and Hyde, a mixed-up kid, having both dignity, because I was created and have been recreated in the image of God, and depravity, because I still have a fallen and rebellious nature. I am both noble and ignoble, beautiful and ugly, good and bad, upright and twisted, image and child of God, and yet sometimes yielding obsequious homage to the devil from whose clutches Christ has rescued me. My true self is what I am by creation, which Christ came to redeem, and by calling. My false self is what I am by the fall, which Christ came to destroy..."*[3]

Here, Stott guides us to the same conclusion Paul makes at the end of his meditation on his own divided nature—*"Who will rescue me from this body of death? Thanks be to God through Jesus Christ our Lord!"*[4]

Rescues rarely come from within; so David's prayer, Stott's reality check, and Paul's reminder point the way toward stamping out the embers of competing personalities—a plea to the One—the only One—who can really grant us that undivided heart. As Stott acknowledges, it will not come overnight; and as Paul reminds us, the struggle will likely continue, but calling out to Him is the best hope we have.

---

1   In this case, "fear" is to be understood as respect—placing before God the honor due His name.
2   Romans 7:15.
3   John Stott, *The Cross of Christ* (Downer's Grove: Intervarsity Press, 1986).
4   Romans 7:24–25.

Summer Time

Take just a moment or two and honestly consider where, in your daily living, you divide your personality—when do you find yourself speaking or acting as one person, but knowing you are really another? Do you really want an undivided heart? If you know the rescue can come only from outside you, not within, can you call out to the One who can take the divided heart and make it one?

A Prayer

Ah Lord, to whom all hearts are open, You can pilot the ship of our souls far better than we can. Stand up, Lord, and command the stormy wind and the troubled sea of our hearts to be still, and at peace in You, so that we may look up to you undisturbed, and rest in union with you, our Lord. Do not let us be carried hither and thither by wandering thoughts, but, forgetting all else, let us see and hear You alone. Renew our spirits; kindle in us Your light, that it may shine within us, and our hearts may burn in love and adoration for You. Let your Holy Spirit dwell in us continually, and make us your temples and sanctuary. Fill us with the divine love and light and life, and with devout and heavenly thoughts, with comfort and strength, with joy and peace. Amen.

— John Arndt, d. 1621

Deserted Times

"Then Jesus was led up by the Spirit into the wilderness to be tempted by the devil. He fasted forty days and forty nights, and afterwards he was famished."

— Matthew 4:1-2

....

For what do you hunger when you are alone?

When I was a much younger man, a friend and I set out to hike a small portion of the Appalachian Trail. We had some idea of where we wanted to enter the trail, but had to drive to a certain spot. Before long, paved road turned to gravel, and then gravel to dirt road. It was nearly midnight before we decided just to stop in the middle of what appeared to be an abandoned road. We set up a tent, made a fire, and after a long talk went to sleep in a place that appeared to be in the middle of nowhere, a deserted place, waiting for what the sun's rising might bring.

One reason for offering a collection of meditations is to encourage the reader to step away from the constancy of life's pace and to "retreat" from all that is common in day-to-day life. It is not uncommon to resist such a retreat. In seminary, I took a three-day private retreat within a monastic community in rural Maryland. When I met with the spiritual director at the beginning of my retreat, I was told the first twenty-four hours were to be spent in complete silence, in prayer, and in fasting. For one who spends much of his time around other people engaging in conversation, a day without speaking seemed like a daunting task indeed!

However, we learn a lot from those deserted times, do we not? When we are really quiet and at the same time, really listen—whether it be to belly growl, or heart's beat, or mind's thought, there is usually a message to be heard.

The first thing Jesus did after His baptism was to go to His own deserted place—in this case, the desert itself. Luke tells us He was there for forty days, without food, water, or the comforts of home.[1] While there, He was tempted; but the real point on which to focus here is that Jesus willingly entered that deserted place.[2] One might assume that after his baptism, Jesus might perform a grand miracle or offer a memorable sermon, but clearly the three Gospels all record it almost as if Jesus quietly slipped away from the River Jordan into a place that seemed like utter abandonment.

It was here, free from the trappings of adoring or threatening crowds, away from the satiation that comes with food and drink, removed from any task whatsoever, that Jesus could come face to face with life's deepest needs, and the rich offering to those needs.

When my daughter was young, I took her to a *New Kids on the Block* concert. I am no old fogey, but it seemed like the loudest music I had ever heard; and when we left, my ears literally rang for hours. It took a long time, with no sound at all, before my hearing settled back to normal. Virtually every other aspect of our lives can be like that—we can eat so much as to not be able to hold another bite, regardless of how good the next bite might be; we can exercise so much that we cannot take another step; we can talk so much that our vocal chords become hoarse and weak; we can stare at the bright light of a computer or television screen so long that our real vision is skewed when we turn away.

On the other hand, of course, when we draw away from what may deafen us, blind us, exhaust us, we often find in those deserted quiet places the strength to meet another day. Jesus used His forty days alone to set the stage for what would be three years of ministry, which was so extraordinary that we are still talking about it today. What might happen if you consciously chose to step away....really step away...and see what the silence says to you?

Back to the Appalachian Trail. When the sun came up on my friend and me, we heard the distant sound of feet pattering on the ground. As it got closer and closer, we unzipped our tent and looked out only to find a jogger coming through the woods...right down the same road we thought was a virtual dead end to our destination! A turn or two on our part, and we were ready to set out on our real journey. Maybe deserted places are not so deserted after all?

---

1   See Mark's version, 1:12–13; and Luke's, 4:1–13.
2   I will touch on the temptation part in the next meditation.

Summer Time

How can you, today, choose to retreat to a deserted place? It can be as simple as a few moments of prayer in a familiar chair or as intensive as making plans today to journey to a place that offers silent retreats. Why not be still for a moment or two, and then, choose to welcome deserted places?

A Prayer

O my divine Master, teach me to hold myself in silence before You, to adore You in the depths of my being, to wait upon You always and never to ask anything of You but the fulfillment of Your will. Teach me to let You act in my soul, and form in it the simple prayer that says little but includes everything. Grant me this favor for the glory of Your name.

— John Arndt, d. 1621

Hungering for Something More

"...he was famished. The tempter came and said to him, 'If you are the Son of God, command these stones to become loaves of bread.' But he answered, 'It is written: 'One does not live by bread alone, but by every word that comes from the mouth of God.'"

— Matthew 4:2-4

....

With what do you feed your deepest hungers?

A real treat for me during my childhood years was a trip to the state fair or traveling circus. I remember a wide variety of experiences to enliven the senses, but cannot leave out perhaps the most memorable—the food. It was food we did not eat on any normal basis—corndogs dipped in ketchup, thick salty pretzels slathered with mustard, funnel cakes sprinkled with powdered sugar; and, of course, cotton candy in a wide variety of colors.

Cotton candy must be one of the most unusual of all sweet treats—a moment of sweetness on the lips and tongue, but with no nutritional value to feed the body and no substance to feed one's hunger. Additional bites might bring a sense of carbohydrate saturation, but cotton candy will not really fill the tummy.

Cotton candy may also be one of the most metaphoric of the food groups—for there are many, many experiences in life that may give momentary delight, but do not really fill our deepest needs. On the surface, we see this played out rather liberally in human culture—healthy eating shifts to gluttony, social drinking to alcoholism, sexual experimentation replaces authentic intimacy, a healthy work ethic gives way to voracious ambition. There is nothing intrinsically wrong with food, drink, sex, or work—it is when any of these is transformed as a "food source" for the soul that things get out of whack.

We know that after Jesus' forty days and nights, He was hungry. So when the tempter made his first attack to try and sidetrack the soon-to-be public Messiah, he made a run at the most obvious target—physical hunger. Jesus knew better. Jesus did not play into the game. "No...you know, humans are not nourished by bread alone, in fact, Satan, they are really nourished from the words that come from the mouth of God." That is a show-stopper. There was not much of a response the tempter could make to that, and none is recorded.

Jesus was making a profound statement. He did not diminish the value of physical bread, noting that humans do, in fact, live by such bread; it is just that they do not live by that bread alone—there is a greater bread. Jesus talked a lot about bread. He suggested that we should pray for daily bread; He used bread as the enduring symbol of His body to be offered for the sake of humankind; and He, in fact, called Himself, "the bread of life."[1] By telling His followers to pray for bread to nourish the body, He was affirming our vital need for bread in our daily living; but by calling Himself the bread of life, Jesus was pointing the way to nourishment for eternal living.

It is important that we understand this juxtaposition. Bread is good, but it does not last; if left uneaten it molds and become useless, and even when eaten, it eventually is completely digested and becomes waste that leaves the body. When we grab hold of things not meant to last and put them in their wrongful place; then we will, in time, find ourselves not just disappointed, but utterly without nourishment.

How many times have we read a news story about someone who seems, from the outside looking in, to "have it all;" and yet they collapse into addiction, destructive behavior or even suicide. It may

---

1   Matthew 6:11; 26:26; John 6:41, 48, 51.

seem baffling until we really think about it. All the money, power, physical pleasure, and fame in the world cannot make up for a life devoid of God.

Cultural philosopher and English columnist Bernard Levin named this truth while writing about his own nation:

> *"Countries like ours are full of people who have all the material comforts they desire, together with such non-material blessings as a happy family, and yet lead lives of quiet, and at times noisy, desperation, understanding nothing but the fact that there is a hole inside them and that however much food and drink they pour into it, however many motor cars and television sets they stuff it with, however many well balanced children and loyal friends they parade around the edges of it...it aches."[2]*

Jesus' answer to the tempter speaks directly to this ache. We can easily, foolishly, pour away our lives into ventures that are nothing more than spiritual wastelands. There is a wonderful old story that helps us understand this just a bit better.

I have always been moved by the story of a little lad in the early 1900s who lived far out in the country. He had reached the age of

twelve and had never in all his life seen a circus. Therefore, you can imagine his excitement one day when a poster went up at school that the next Saturday a traveling circus was coming to a nearby town. He ran home with the glad news and then came the question, "Daddy, can I go?" The family was poor, but the father could see how much this meant to his boy so he said, "If you will do your Saturday chores ahead of time, I'll see to it that you have the money to go."

Come Saturday morning, the chores were done and the little boy stood dressed in his Sunday best by the breakfast table. His father reached down in his overalls and pulled out a

---

2   Nicky Gumbel, *Questions of Life* (Colorado Springs: Cook Communications Ministries, 2003), 13–14.

dollar bill—the most money the little boy has ever seen at one time in all his life. The father cautioned him to be careful and then sent him on his way to town. He was so excited his feet hardly seemed to touch the ground all the way. As he got to the outskirts of the village, he noticed that people were lining the streets and he worked his way through the crowd until he could see what was coming. And there, lo and behold, in the distance approached the spectacle of a circus parade!

It was the grandest thing this lad had ever beheld. There were animals in cages and bands and gymnasts and all that goes on to make up such a show. Finally, at the end of the parade, the traditional circus clown, with floppy shoes and baggy pants and brightly painted face, came bringing up the rear.

As the clown passed where he was standing, the little boy reached into his pocket and got out that precious dollar bill. Handing the money to the clown, the boy then turned around and went home. What had happened? *The boy thought he had seen the circus, when he had only seen the parade!*

We do not find cotton candy just at the county fair or circus. It is certainly a nice treat from time to time—just do not mistake it for a real meal, and when that meal is done, remember—humans do not live by bread alone, but by feeding on the One who is the Bread of everlasting life.

 Summer Time

In the last meditation, we looked at the hungers that speak to us when we are quiet. Now take a moment and ponder this question: With what do you feed those hungers? Where can you rid yourself of cotton-candy solutions to bread of life hungers?

A Prayer

I am so very hungry dear Lord,
so very hungry;
Not for food that settles the stomach,
but bread that heals my wounds.

I thirst, ah Jesus,
I thirst,
Not for drink to wet my lips,
but wine that fills my soul.

I long, my God,
I long;
Not to be held, or told, or even embraced,
but to know peace in my heart.

Feed me, dear Lord,
And fill me Jesus, fill me;
That my deepest need is met,
perfectly and wholly
In nothing more,
than You.
Amen.

"It's Not What You Know..."

"As Jesus passed along the Sea of Galilee, he saw Simon and his brother Andrew casting a net into the sea—for they were fishermen. And Jesus said to them, 'Follow me and I will make you fish for people.' And immediately they left their nets and followed him."

— Mark 1:16-18

Whom do you follow?

While I have learned a few things on my own, most of what I have learned of value has come from following someone else's lead. In my leisure hours, this particularly applies to my fishing skills.

I have a friend who is a boat captain. We have now been fishing on a number of occasions, but I would know very little about where to fish, how best to cast, hook and reel in, without the knowledge I have gained by having him stand over my shoulder, and at times even taking the reel and rod in hand with me. One can learn a great deal

from books, and even more from personal experience, but rarely does someone become all they can be without someone by their side who will help them along the way.

This scene from Mark gives a snapshot of the Jesus recruitment technique. I suggest it is a snapshot, because I suspect there was more going on. Word about Jesus had no doubt gotten around. Simon and Andrew had likely seen and listened to Jesus in some setting other than by the Sea of Galilee. Perhaps they had already been considering leaving the lives they knew for a life about which, at that point, they knew very little.[1] So with that possible prelude, along comes Jesus, catching them in "mid-cast," with three words that had the potential to change their lives forever: *"Come, follow me."*

When an itinerant rabbi in Jesus' day invited others to follow, it did not mean, "Follow me for a little conversation," or "Follow me to the synagogue," nor did it mean "Follow me for a few days." No, when an invitation like this was shared, it meant "Follow me to a way of life." Specifically, Jesus was inviting these "first to follow" to share meals, discussion, prayers, questions, laughter, tears, frustration, joy, and in the following, to learn from Him how best to journey through all of life's offering.

For years, the rolling stone who was Jesus Christ would pick up followers. He began with a few and expanded His inner circle to twelve, but of course there were many more. As to what knowledge those first twelve possessed with regard to the faith and the Lord they would be following before they met Jesus, God only knows; but clearly, in order to be true followers, it had to be not just a matter of the head, but of the heart; not just of the lips, but of the lives.

We all remember the saying, "You are what you eat," meaning your physical constitution is based in large part upon the food you consume. The same is true about the people we become as it relates to heart and soul. Becoming who you want to be, or for Christians, who God wants you to be, is not so much about what you know as whom you follow.

Some may say, "It really does not matter whom you follow, as long as that person is earnest and sincere in their beliefs." No doubt, Hitler, Pol Pot, Amin were earnest and sincere in their beliefs. No, it *does* matter whom you follow, if you intend to get somewhere in particular.

For Christians, we likely struggle with following Jesus as we should. There are so many distractions that can cause us to veer off that journey. I once saw a sculpture many years ago by the artist and Episcopal priest, Craig Biddle. The carving showed Simon, head and

---

1   I confess this is conjecture on my part.

eyes strained toward an unseen Jesus who is calling him to follow, but Simon's hands are still holding onto the nets of his daily trade. Clearly Simon wants to let go and follow, but this is the moment in which his mind and heart are struggling together to decide whether or not to fully follow. Of course, we know Simon released those nets, but Biddle's interpretation is, for my money, much closer to what might have really happened in that crucial moment.

Of course, Jesus had a goal for those who followed, *"I will make you fish for people."* Leaving one set of nets behind meant taking up another kind. Leaving one life behind meant taking on another. But the point is, the early apostles became who they ultimately were created to be because when it came time to choose who to follow, they followed Jesus. Maybe they did it *"at once,"* as the Bible says, but maybe that *"at once"* was not so much a matter of time as it was of timing—for at the right time, they chose to belong to Jesus and they learned to cast nets that drew myriads into the grace and love of God.

Author Parker Palmer reminds us;

> *"The Quaker teacher Douglas Steere was fond of saying that the ancient human question 'Who am I?' leads inevitably to the equally important question 'Whose am I?'—for there is no selfhood outside of relationship. We must ask the question of selfhood and answer it as honestly as we can, no matter where it takes us...."*[2]

Jesus' invitation to follow, is really an invitation to asks Steere's question, *"Whose am I?"*

I learned how to fish by giving myself over to my good friend, who knew how to fish so much better than I. As to living as a child of God, I have found the same is so very true of when I give myself over to Jesus.

Indeed, it is not what you know, but whom you follow. Well?

---

2   Parker Palmer, *Let Your Life Speak* (San Francisco: Jossey-Bass, 2000), 17.

Summer Time

So now, who or what do you follow? If it is a hard question to answer, consider what Ralph Waldo Emerson once wrote, "A man is what he thinks about all day long," which, of course, is another way of saying, "You are what you eat..." You become, in a very real way, "who" or "what" you follow. So what do you think about all day long? What does it say about who you follow? Is it time to leave a particular net behind so you can pick the one Jesus would have you use?

A Prayer

We pray to You, O Lord, Who are the supreme Truth, and all truth is from You. We beseech You, O Lord, Who are the highest Wisdom, and all the wise depend on You for their wisdom. You are the supreme Joy, and all who are happy owe it to You. You are the highest Good, and all goodness comes from You. You are the Light of minds, and all receive their understanding from You. We love you—indeed we love You above all things. We seek You, follow You and are prepared to serve You. We desire to dwell under Your power, for You are the King of all. Amen.

— King Alfred the Great of Wessex, d. 849

"And when you pray..."

"And whenever you pray, do not be like the hypocrites; for they love to stand and pray in the synagogues and at the street corners, so that they may be seen by others. Truly I tell you, they have received their reward. But whenever you pray, go into your room and shut the door and pray to your Father who is in secret; and your Father who sees in secret will reward you. When you are praying, do not heap up empty phrases as the Gentiles do; for they think that they will be heard because of their many words. Do not be like them, for your Father knows what you need before you ask him."

— Matthew 6:5-8

How do you pray?

You may be one of the fortunate ones who has come across a sand dollar. If it was dead, the "skeleton" it leaves behind is quite lovely—a circle, typically with five small eyelet holes, and a "star" design in the center. If it was alive, and you decided to keep it, you might have soaked it in bleach to get the same effect, (to the detriment of the sand dollar I must add!). I own several of both kinds, of various sizes, and most of them carry a memory or two.

Some I had gathered did not make their way to my display. Once, when snorkeling with some friends, we came upon a seabed literally covered with live sand dollars. Not dozens, not even hundreds, but thousands. I had never seen anything like it before, nor have I since. I was a young man at the time and failed to know both the folly and the waste of hoarding. I grabbed and bagged as many as I could and brought them back to the shore. Over the next few days, I tried to bleach them, but because there were so many, the bleach could not do its job. The "pile" of dying echinoderms were causing a stench and the chemicals were not strong enough to eat their way through all the debris.

If I had only chosen one or two to bring back and treat, they no doubt would be sitting on my shelves today with the others. Alas, my gluttony for the treasures meant the whole experience was a waste.

I am a preacher by trade, and words are the tools of that trade. But perhaps no fewer words have been spoken than that gentle, though instructive, quip, *"Less is more."* This is in part what Jesus instructs His audience with regard to prayer.

His points are clear. First, Jesus does not implore prayer, He assumes it. *"When you pray,"* is how he begins the teaching. Prayer was not an option for His followers—it was part of the life of being a follower of Jesus. That has not changed. Richard Foster reminds us that among our forebears, *"prayer was no little habit tacked onto the periphery of their lives; it was their lives."[1]*

Second, Jesus asks that when praying, we not be like hypocrites— as ones who *pretend* to pray. It was very common in Jesus' time for people who wanted to be admired for their piety to perform those same acts in public, so as to win the praise of those who see them. For those who choose to pray like this, Jesus says, they get the reward they really wanted—simply, the applause of their audience, who in this case, happens not to be God.

Third, Jesus instructs us to pray for the audience of One. Go into a private place, and there—let your prayers be earnest, to the point, and without all the falderal of pretentious language and wordiness.

---

1   Foster, *Celebration of Discipline*, 34.

Pagans babble; His followers get to the point. Why? Because, fourth, God is going to give you what you need. With prayer, it seems, less is more.

I remember praying with a parishioner many years ago who was going through a horrible time in his marriage. We bowed our heads, closed our eyes, and then I addressed God in a personal way, asked God to help my friend in his pain and to heal his marriage. *Amen.* That was about it. When we finished, he looked at me and said, "I did not know you could pray like that." "Like what?" I said. "No Thees or Thous...and you just laid it out there...you just told Him what we needed." "That's prayer," I told him, "Why waste any time? Get to the point."

This may raise a point for us. If God knows what we need, why bother? Well, prayer is not so much about getting your grocery list of things dropped in your lap as it is about relationship. Prayer is the communication channel between you and God. If you are married or have close friends, they likely know "what you want" before you ask them; but think of what happens when you go days, or even weeks, without speaking. Think of what that lack of communication does to the depth of your relationship. Prayer to and with (since we are told the Holy Spirit often helps us in our prayers!) God deepens our relationship with Him. It also opens the door to deeper prayers that are not so much about getting what we want, but perhaps getting what God wants for us.

I learned the hard way that a big old pile of rotting sand dollars was not near as precious as just a few. Maybe take some time today, to tell God what you need—and remember, less is more.

Summer Time

If you could write your needs down with just three words today—what would those words be? When you pray, do you seek the applause of many, or pray just to an audience of One? Close your door, get still and quiet, pray to your heavenly Father, Who knows what you need before you even ask—but ask anyway.

A Prayer

Lord Jesus,
Friend and Savior,
here I am,
simply me.
Cracks and broken places I bring,
wants to my liking,
and needs I know not yet.
As You know, and know already,
how best to answer my prayer,
give me a ready heart,
open hands,
and humble soul,
to receive with joy,
Your gifts to me.
Amen.

Doling It Out

"Do not judge, and you will not be judged; do not condemn, and you will not be condemned. Forgive, and you will be forgiven; give, and it will be given to you. A good measure, pressed down, shaken together, running over, will be put into your lap; for the measure you give will be the measure you get back."

— Luke 6:37-38

Do you give as you would like to receive?

During seminary training, we lived minutes away from downtown Washington, D.C. If you know the city, you will know that most of the museums, exhibits, and monuments are open and free of charge to anyone willing to meet the challenges of parking and crowds—particularly depending on the time of day. I have to confess, I found the sweet spot around 3 p.m. on Friday.

While I was in class, my wife held down part-time jobs and tended to a wide array of duties connected with two young children. So there were times blocked out that parental duty was mine and mine alone. We could leave our apartment and only moments away be parking right on D.C.'s famous mall, with the Lincoln Memorial looking toward the Washington Monument facing the United States Capitol and Smithsonian Museum, incredible buildings lining either side for nearly two miles. We would arrive, park, I would let the kids choose one of Smithsonian's many options (Natural History, American, African, Air and Space, etc.) where we would spend an hour or two—and, well, it was all free. Of course, I am well aware that when I pay tax, a portion goes to support this ongoing "free fest," but given the benefit I received from nearly three years of touring these great places along our National Mall, I always felt like what my family received

was far more than we deserved based on whatever meager contribution we were making.

Jesus speaks very pointedly about giving and receiving in the above passage from Luke, but it has more to do with how we live with others than how we might spend a day at the museum. In this instance, He speaks of judging, forgiving and giving to others. *"A good measure,"* Jesus says *"running over"* will be *"poured into your lap."* In ancient Palestine, it was common for an outer garment of clothing to be worn in a specific way that left a fold over one's belt—thereby creating a very large pocket to hold a *"measure"* of wheat.

We know that virtually all we experience in the way of gifts from God are the fruit of grace—a free gift; but Jesus also reminds us that often in our human relationships we should act and live as we would wish to be treated. Several times in Scripture, we are enjoined to *"love your neighbor as yourself."*[1] We do this, not because we win any points with God—not because we have to, but because we want to; it is a natural Christian ethic to treat another as you wish to be treated.

To "dole" something out is to administer, divide up, and give away. When it comes to doling out the virtues of our faith, Jesus always seems to be pressing us to go the extra mile...forget about what you think you deserve, give in huge ways, give without an expectation you will receive anything back, give lavishly and abundantly, and, well, Jesus says you will receive a full measure in return.

In doing so, you may feel like you are having to ante up to play in the game of human relationships, (i.e. you may give and not get back what you think you deserve); but oftentimes, perhaps more often

---

1   Leviticus 19:18; Matthew 19:19 for instance.

than not, you get back more than you ever imagined. Choosing to hold back from condemning and judging another, choosing to recklessly forgive, is the conscious act of mindlessly giving yourself to another. And Jesus is clear, the way you dole it out is the way it will be doled out to you. If that is the case, why not dole it out, without ifs, ands, or buts; without parameters, provisos or restrictions, just give it away—and see how freely the gifts come back to you—so freely, that my bet is, you will feel it is beyond your deserving—but it is not, you know.

When my kids and I finished up our little museum tours on Friday, we always visited the merry-go-round right in front of the Smithsonian Castle (the first of the Smithsonian buildings). That was usually the only thing that we actually paid for—about 50 cents a head, if memory serves.

The amusement ride was run by a small circle of friends we got to know over the years. On that very last Friday before we moved away, I brought them a plate full of cookies my wife had made and thanked them for all the memories they gave to my children and me. My friend in the ticket booth smiled and printed out several sets of tickets for which we did not pay, allowing us not one ride, but several. We rode and rode the rest of the afternoon, using tickets for which we did not pay, but which had been doled out to us in a good, full, measure.

 Summer Time

Let's really be honest for a moment. Do you treat others as you would like to be treated? Take some extra time and read Matthew 5:43-48. Here Jesus tells us to go the extra mile by extending our love well beyond the boundaries of what "everyone else" is doing. Since that is the case, who in your circle of human relationships needs you to dole out just a bit more charity, grace, forgiveness, love?

A Prayer

Oh Lord God Almighty, Giver of every good gift;
as you have been generous with me;
may I, by the power of Your Spirit,
be generous with all you send my way.

Unhinge me when I desire to close doors;
empty me when I am tempted to hoard;
release me when I ache for fear of letting go;
free me when am bound up.

And finally by Your mercy, birth within me that
great truth that it is in giving we receive;
in serving we are more faithful;
and in loving others that we are
most like Your Son;

Who gave, and served and loved,
that we might find ourselves in doing the same.
for His Name's sake,
and for the sake of Your Kingdom,
grant this my prayer.

Amen.

Doing the Right Thing

"One sabbath he was going through the grainfields; and as they made their way his disciples began to pluck heads of grain. The Pharisees said to him, 'Look, why are they doing what is not lawful on the sabbath?' And he said to them, 'Have you never read what David did when he and his companions were hungry and in need of food? He entered the house of God, when Abiathar was high priest, and ate the bread of the Presence, which it is not lawful for any but the priests to eat, and he gave some to his companions.' Then he said to them, 'The sabbath was made for humankind, and not humankind for the sabbath.'"

— Mark 2:23-27

....

How do you judge the greater good?

For the most part, the laws of nature seem fairly clear. The law of gravity will cause an apple to drop from a tree, and keep the earth in its orbit. The laws of nature work together to bring forth birth or bring about death. With the exception of domesticated animals, interaction between animals and humans is not the norm. There are, however, times when these laws are breached.

I once spent virtually an entire day scuba diving with large herds of manatees in Crystal River, Florida.[1] The creatures are large, and while some may say they are a bit clumsy, they are really more docile. Those that migrate to the same areas year after year have grown accustomed to human visitors and it is not uncommon to have these cows of the sea approach out of curiosity, and some will actually allow a pat on the head or scratch on the back.

---

1 For the most part, scuba diving is no longer allowed where manatees migrate, though visitors may snorkel with the creatures in controlled areas.

I was fortunate to have an even greater rare moment as I approached a mother and her calf. Mother was probably close to eight feet long, the calf much smaller. Neither swam away, and as I gently approached, clearly mom was "on guard," but she allowed for my frivolity. The calf approached, and at first allowed for a gentle stroke or two, but as we spent more time together, it actually rolled over onto its back and allowed a full tummy rub. Mother floated nearby and allowed this unusual play between mammals to continue for a few minutes, but then, as if she were saying "Time's up" to two children on the playground, she gently moved over to the calf and gave it a little bump. It turned, snuggled up against Mom and the two swam away. It was a brief "break" in the laws of nature, but for a few moments, we were both the better for it.

Perhaps it is contrary to the familiar quip, but laws were not made to be broken. As my reader probably knows, the great laws of the Old Testament were summed up in the Ten Commandments that were given to Moses on Mount Sinai.[2] But over time they were expanded to over 600 various laws, about a third being positive laws (what to do) and the remaining being negative (what not to do). Of course, over time, these laws were interpreted in a wide variety of ways, and the faith they were supposed to enhance became in some circles an intricate and restrictive religious system by which one won favor with God, (i.e. keeping the law was good, failing to do so was bad). The problem with this thinking is that the faith then became focused far more on the rules than the Rule-Maker.

As Jesus came on the scene and unveiled the possibility of relationship with God unfettered by legalistic rule-keeping, some believed He was handing out hall passes for unjustified truancy. He was quick to respond, *"I have not come to abolish [the law], but to fulfill [it]."*[3] In some sense, it seems, Jesus even made the law more restrictive. He told His listeners that though they had heard they were not to commit adultery, Jesus would take it further and say that lust in the heart is equal to adultery of the body. Where some believed only physical violence against another was unlawful, Jesus would say violent thoughts are just as bad.[4]

On the other hand, we see Jesus consistently, throughout His earthly ministry, bumping up against the various laws, as in the Scripture at the beginning of this meditation. According to Jewish tradition, work of any sort was forbidden on the Sabbath.[5] Those who spotted Jesus' disciples

---

2 See Exodus 20:1–17.
3 See Matthew 5:17–20.
4 See Matthew 5:21–30.
5 See Exodus 34:21.

picking grain on the Sabbath deemed them lawbreakers. Jesus did not dismiss their concerns, but used the opportunity to remind them that the law is there to serve its maker, and not the other way around. He pointed them to the time when David and his companions ate consecrated bread, and while this also was unlawful, it is always lawful to do good. David was acting in accordance with the spirit of the law; he was not rejecting the validity of the law, but choosing a greater good for the good of his friends.

Jesus took the law seriously, but He (and He alone by the way) was able to "be" the living law. We see, in Jesus, what the "law" really looks like. For Jesus, choosing the greater good within the spirit of the law at times trumped the letter of the law. This was, of course, the exception, not the rule.

Jesus was not proposing circumstantial morality or situational ethics, but He was always pushing His followers to look for the deeper meaning of the law—doing good as a fruit of that right relationship with God. At times, it seems, that even included stepping across some rather well-defined barriers.

I was fortunate to benefit from a brief breaking of the laws of nature those many years ago in a brief encounter in a lagoon off the coast of central Florida; but it reminded me that the law was meant to serve, not to be served.

There is a final caveat here. Jesus ends this little teaching with a bold claim: that in the end, He is actually the Lord of the Sabbath. That means Sabbath rules—and in fact all rules as they apply to our relationship with God and one another—should be guided by Jesus and His greatest law, love of the other, a law that trumps all others.

Summer Time

I realize offering this meditation is opening a small can of worms. There is a slippery slope in suggesting laws are, at times, to be broken for the greater good, because anyone could define good to their own advantage and thus break the rules with the same motive. However, Jesus' teaching, and frankly model, suggests that such an ethic only applies when it is for the good of the other, not the self. With that in mind, is there someone in your life, right now, today, that needs you to operate more out of the spirit of the law than its letter? To serve him or her out of the great law of love over and above the law of the books? Take that dilemma to Jesus and let Him guide you to the perfect law.

A Prayer

Grant to me, O Lord, to know what I ought to know, to love what I ought to love, to praise what delights You most, to value what is precious in Your sight, to hate what is offensive to You. Do not suffer me to judge according to the sight of my eyes nor to pass sentence according to the hearing of ignorant men; but to discern with true judgment between things visible and spiritual and above all things to inquire what is the good pleasure of your will. Amen.

— Thomas à Kempis, d. 1471

Listen Up!

"Now about eight days after these sayings Jesus took with him Peter and John and James, and went up on the mountain to pray. And while he was praying, the appearance of his face changed, and his clothes became dazzling white. Suddenly they saw two men, Moses and Elijah, talking to him. They appeared in glory and were speaking of his departure, which he was about to accomplish at Jerusalem. Now Peter and his companions were weighed down with sleep; but since they had stayed awake, they saw his glory and the two men who stood with him. Just as they were leaving him, Peter said to Jesus, 'Master, it is good for us to be here; let us make three dwellings, one for you, one for Moses, and one for Elijah'— not knowing what he said. While he was saying this, a cloud came and overshadowed them; and they were terrified as they entered the cloud. Then from the cloud came a voice that said, 'This is my Son, my Chosen; listen to him!' When the voice had spoken, Jesus was found alone. And they kept silent and in those days told no one any of the things they had seen."

— Luke 9:28-36

....

Are you listening?

It seems almost silly to write, but I seem to learn the most when I am really listening. Hearing is one thing; listening is another. Hearing is the receiving of sound waves that brush against the tympanum of your ear in such ways that sounds make themselves known. You could choose to ignore those sounds. Or you could pay close attention to what they are saying—we call that listening.

Listening can lift a veil such that we hear things to which we may be deaf. But of course the key that unlocks the mystery of the yet-to-be-learned is a willingness to really be still and listen. There is a great little saying—*"God gave us two ears and one mouth for a reason, so that we would listen twice as much as we talk!"*

Museums are good places to practice listening. I have spent a lot of time in them over the years enjoying beautiful paintings, majestic sculptures, startling cast metals and carved woods. Few museums rival The Louvre in Paris, France. When I visited it many years ago, like many other tourists, I made my way to one of its most famous exhibits, DaVinci's *Mona Lisa*. There were literally dozens of tourists crammed together trying to get just a glimpse of her well-known countenance and mysterious smile. But to this day, one of the things that struck me is that most of them were not really looking—they were talking, pointing, laughing, remarking, and some were merely quickly snapping photos and running off to another exhibit. They seemed to be there to look, but not really see.

The scene from Luke's Gospel is called the Transfiguration because of the transformation of Jesus' appearance as He prayed on a mountain and was greeted by Moses and Elijah. Peter was there when it happened, and he was so overwhelmed, we are told he did not pause to take it in, but almost immediately set out to make monuments to the moment because, Luke tells us, Peter really did not know what to say. Then we learn he really should have said nothing.

It is hard to argue with the voice of God—*"This is my Son, my Chosen; listen to him!"* Not "hear Him," but *"listen* to Him." Listening involves not just a physical silence, but an inward silence; a willingness to submit to something other than your own thoughts. When that submission is directed under God's Son—something remarkable can happen. *"If we are silent, who will take control? God will take control,"* writes Richard Foster.[1] Is that not the aim of the Christian life? To let God take control?

Listening in this way requires a kind of true silence, not just quietness, but silence of the noises that can flood not just the ears, but the heart, mind, and soul as well. True silence bids us to put our listening at the disposal of God's voice for the sake of being transformed—perhaps transfigured in our own way, if you will. The Roman Catholic author and social worker Catherine de Hueck Doherty suggested, *"True silence is the key to the immense and flaming heart of God. It is the beginning of a divine courtship that will end only in the immense, creative, fruitful, loving silence of final union with the Beloved."*[2]

Chances are I missed a great deal by walking by too quickly past some of the other exhibits that day in The Louvre; there are over 30,000 paintings alone. But I have wondered what those who did a drive-by of the *Mona Lisa* missed—the bridge and road in the background? The mountains covered with white? Or is that fog? What appears to be the carefully handstitched embroidery of her blouse, the particular drape of her wrap, the carefully and at the same time almost carelessly displayed fingers? One could miss a lot if they are just seeing but not looking.

One could miss a lot by hearing and not listening...so, well, listen up!

---

1   Foster, *Celebration of Discipline*, 101.
2   Martin H. Manser, comp.*The Westminster Collection of Christian Quotations* (London: Westminster John Knox Press, 2001), 342.

Summer Time

Turn off the phone, the television, the music. Quiet the mind, the heart, the soul. Open the ears and listen...you may even hear the very voice of God.

A Prayer

(Begin by taking several deep breaths)

Almighty and everlasting God,
Fountain of all that is true and lovely;
I confess it is hard to be quiet, to listen,
but I ask You to please grant me in this moment
the gift of silence.

Calm now my restlessness,
subdue my busyness,
and give me both an outward hush
and an inward stillness;
That I may not just listen
to my heart's desire,
But Yours for me,
and in listening I may,
by Your grace,
truly hear
Your voice.
Amen.

Kid's Stuff

"People were bringing even infants to him that he might touch them; and when the disciples saw it, they sternly ordered them not to do it. But Jesus called for them and said, 'Let the little children come to me, and do not stop them; for it is to such as these that the kingdom of God belongs. Truly I tell you, whoever does not receive the kingdom of God as a little child will never enter it.'"

— Luke 18:15-17

How might you become more like a child?[1]

Did you ever have that experience as you were growing up when you were out playing with other friends, someone would pop out a

suggestion, and someone in the crowd would be the first to say *"Ah! Come on! That's kid's stuff!"* There is a lot in that little response. It tells us that someone in the crowd is recognizing the natural progression of life—that childhood leads to teen years, teen to adult and so on. And with each progression something of the former is—even should be—left behind. In some sense, noting that "kid's stuff" is not for "grown-ups" is a good thing, but Jesus seems to offer a "not so fast" in this passage from Luke.

---

1   This meditation was written by Laura Levenson.

When His apostles (and in this scene it appears they are taking on the role of ushers) rush in to try and save Jesus from a crowd of young ones, Jesus suggests they hold off a bit. While it is almost as if the apostles were collectively saying "Jesus does not have time for this kid's stuff!" Jesus says in return—"Watch! There's much to learn from these little ones." As usual, He was right, of course.

The amazement of a child is a precious and wondrous thing. We do not have to be a parent to have seen children respond to a new sight or experience. If only we could recapture our first vision of the ocean, or snow, Disneyland, or puppies! When we see things through the lens of a child, with all their innocence and wonder, it is as though we ourselves are reliving those amazing moments and feeling those original emotions.

Jesus loved and loves His "little ones." Children who are taught about God naturally respond to Him and to His Word. They accept without question that Jesus loves them. Their prayers are authentic and encompass their world. That is likely, precisely why Jesus said, *"whoever does not receive the kingdom of God as a little child will never enter it."* That may be a sharp sting, but it is also offers some up-front clarity—accept, believe, live in the way a child does—purely, lovingly, simply, or you will never really understand God's Kingdom.

Would that we might be able to remember what that simple acceptance is like! We adults have so complicated God's message that at times it is hardly recognizable. Any child can tell you the real truth about Jesus. He loves all of us, and we should love Him back!

Today, when you pray, try allowing Jesus to speak to the child within you. Come before Him with wonder. Discover the joy of simply being loved and loving Him back. You are God's child and he loves you. It IS amazing! And it IS wondrous! It may be kid's stuff—but it is also the pathway to the Kingdom of God.

Summer Time

Will you allow God to awaken the child in you again? And in doing so, as that child, can you hear Jesus' tender words, "Let the little children come to me...for it is to such as these that the kingdom of God belongs." Wow.

A Prayer

Now, before I run to play,
Let me not forget to pray,
To God who kept me through the night,
And waked me with the morning light.
Help me, Lord, to love thee more,
Than I have ever loved before,
In my work and in my play,
Be thou with me through the day.
Amen.

—A Traditional Child's Prayer

No Darkness at All

"All things came into being through him, and without him not one thing came into being. What has come into being in him was life, and the life was the light of all people. The light shines in the darkness, and the darkness did not overcome it."

— John 1:3-5

Can you see the light?

I was in sixth grade the first time I visited a planetarium. I will never forget that I found it fascinating. From a very, bright, sunny day, my fellow classmates and I came into an almost pitch black semi-domed auditorium. We were told to sit still for a while and let our eyes adjust, and as we did, much the same way real stars pepper the night sky, little dots of light began

to pop to life, like pinpricks through a black veil. Before long, this faux sky was teeming with life as the curator directed our attention to visiting planets, comets, and meteor showers. Even in that very dark place, there was far more light than we could have ever imagined.

It is sometimes hard to see God when things seem dark. John, our most poetic of Gospel writers, loves to use metaphors throughout his work to unveil the deeper mysteries of the Almighty. But in the passage above, we are given an essential quality of the essence of God—light.

Of course, in virtually every religion since the dawn of time, darkness is associated with evil, as light is with good. But here John reminds us that all things, literally, came into being through the One who is the Light of all people; a light that darkness can never quench.

 When I have been in some of the dark places of my leisure activities, I have always appreciated a good flashlight—when I was diving at ninety feet at the bottom of an underwater cave or through the sunken wreck of the *Balboa* just off Grand Cayman, when my tent and sleeping bag was being soaked wet by a driving rain in the deep woods of a camping trip in south Tennessee, or simply on a long walk around campus during my days as a college chaplain. Flashlights are certainly helpful when you are battling physical darkness, but they are not much help when it comes to spiritual darkness.

All kinds of things can bring spiritual darkness—mental or emotional distress brought on by despair or grief, a sense of hopelessness that is born of an act of betrayal or overwhelming disappointment. The pain another inflicts on you can cause such distress, as can, simply, the evil forces of this world, both seen and unseen. St. John of the Cross called his own battle with spiritual darkness his *Dark Night of the Soul*. We have all had those moments, I suspect. I know I have.

When they come, it is helpful, perhaps even essential, to remember that darkness never, ever comes from God. God does not purposely visit us with evil. God is light—pure light. All that came into being came as a result of His light. When we are journeying through dark times, it may be very, very hard to believe there will ever be light again.

My mentor, John Claypool, once wrote,

> *"Our assumptions are all-important when it comes to how we deal with the facts in the world around us. We are not purely rational, objective creatures. What we end up with as a conclusion is going to be deeply colored by what we begin with as an assumption, and this applies as much to our relationship with God as it does to any other aspect of our existence. The crucial thing here is not simply what God does or does not do in history, but whether our starting point is one of trust or mistrust. That beginning assumption can make all the difference."*[1]

---

1 Claypool, *The Light Within You*, 16.

To take Claypool's words to heart, if we begin with an assumption that darkness only begets more darkness, then in the end, we will only see darkness. But if we begin with the assumption that *"light shines in the darkness, and the darkness did not overcome it,"* then even when we are in the blackest of nights, we will hope for, and may even see, light.

John would later write, *"This is the message we have heard from him and proclaim to you, that God is light and in him there is no darkness at all."*[2] What a precious promise that is! It is literally a lantern in hand when you are in your own dark night of the soul. Hold on to that one.

 Summer Time

What might you be experiencing now that seems it is devoid of the Light of God? It may take a while to get your night vision, but lay your dark place before Him now and see if there is any light; and if you cannot see it, then take it to Jesus, remembering His comforting words, "I am the light of the world. Whoever follows me will never walk in darkness but will have the light of life." — John 8:12

---

2   I John 1:5.

A PRAYER

O Gracious Light
O gracious Light,
pure brightness of the everliving Father in heaven,
O Jesus Christ, holy and blessed!
Now as we come to the setting of the sun
and our eyes behold the vesper light,
we sing your praises,O God: Father, Son, and Holy Spirit.
You are worthy at all times to be praised by happy voices,
O Son of God, O Giver of life,
and to be glorified through all the worlds.[3]
Amen.

---

[3]   Also known as *Phos hilaron.* "Daily Evening Prayer," in *The Prayer Book and Hymnal* (New York: The Church Hymnal Corporation), 112.

Good Wine

*"When the steward tasted the water that had become wine,
and did not know where it came from (though the servants
who had drawn the water knew), the steward called the
bridegroom and said to him, 'Everyone serves the good
wine first, and then the inferior wine after the guests have
become drunk. But you have kept the good wine until now.'
Jesus did this, the first of his signs, in Cana of Galilee, and
revealed his glory; and his disciples believed in him."*

— John 2:9-11

Are you full of care with His gifts?

One of those side trips with our grandmother was sparked by a small
newspaper article she had read. It seemed that a farmer in a nearby
county had a large hornet's nest built *onto* a window. It started as a
small work, perhaps by just a few hornets, drawn by the afternoon
heat or the shade of the day, but eventually it encompassed nearly

the entire window. As an experience for her
grandkids this was a must.

We drove for an hour or so, and as we did
Grantzy kept talking about what we would
likely see. *"Isn't God's creation a strange
thing!"* Indeed, we thought. As we arrived,
she (as usual) knocked on the door. The
agreeable farmer let us in and took us to a
back room of his house. There, as if painted
onto four symmetrical window panes,
was a buzzing, humming mass of hornets

moving in and among the carefully crafted cells and channels of the nest. In some sense, we felt protected by the glass window, in another, it simply gave us the creeps!

After seeing the nest from the inside, we went around to the outside of the house. From the outside, the large nest appeared to be nothing more than a kind of attached, grey pumpkin. There was a small hole toward the bottom from which, and to which, the hornets would come and go. We could even get rather close, without any danger.

Now obviously, had we broken the glass from within or whacked the nest from without, what seemed to be a serene experience from a nature program would have turned sour, painful, and even dangerous. Hold that thought for a moment.

Jesus chose a wedding in Cana of Galilee to perform His first miracle—the changing of water to wine. Let us make no bones about it—it was wine— real wine, laden with some measure of alcohol, though no doubt a low content by today's standards. It is interesting that wine, as a beverage, is mentioned several times in the Old and New Testament. Wine was the symbol Jesus used to remind His followers, in His day and ours, of the price paid for our sins.[1] Paul actually endorsed wine's medicinal qualities, counseling his protégé Timothy to not limit himself to water, but to drink wine because of some stomach ailment.[2] Verses like this—from celebratory to symbolic to medicinal—seem to tell us that drinking wine is a safe bet, if not heartily endorsed by Scripture.

That said, we know from other places in Scripture that our story holds the line at excess. If you are looking for insight from the Bible on where not to cross the line when it comes to enjoying the fruit of the vine, you will find plenty.[3]

At this point in our collection of meditations, we are not going to lean too heavily in one direction or another—what we are going to

---

1   See Luke 22:17–23; Matthew 26:26–29; Mark 14:22–25; I Corinthians 11:23–25.
2   See I Timothy 5:23.
3   I Samuel 1:13, Proverb 23:21; 26:9; Luke 21:34; Romans 13:13; I Corinthians 5:11, 6:10; Galatians 5:21; I Timothy 3:3; I Peter 4:3.

suggest is that our Judeo-Christian story is one that celebrates *all* of God's good gifts, but also always counsels proper stewardship. As we should not make anything God, but God; gifts from God should not become the beating heart of our daily lives. God gives us good food to enjoy, but not with the intent that we will become gluttons; sleep to refresh, but with the hope we will not become lazy or slothful; work to occupy, but not to possess; sex to provide intimacy and pleasure, but not to spin out of control; and God even gives wine to drink, but not to become a hornet's nest of sour, dangerous, painful living. All good gifts of God are to be enjoyed but, taken to the extreme, can spoil as well.

We all know the saying *"All things in moderation..."* There is another good saying, *"All things in moderation, even moderation!"* Our challenge, as followers and imitators of Christ, is to find that godly balance. For some, that means abstention from one thing or another; for others, not so—either way, the journey's end is to experience what the steward at that party in Cana found to be *"good wine,"* wine of Jesus' own making.

That hornet's nest was a work of nature—built by God's creatures. In and of itself, it meant no harm to anyone. Because of where it was built you could actually get close enough to almost touch it, but the veil between safety and danger was thin indeed. Fortunately, we got to see both sides—the good and the bad.

Our story gives us the same opportunity—to see the good, the bad and the in-between. With God's help, we can learn to appreciate the gifts without depreciating the recipient. Drink indeed—just make sure it is of God's own making.

 *Summer Time*

Consider now any area of your life that was intended as gift, but which now may have spun out of control. Perhaps something that used to bring joy has now become an addiction, a relationship that once was meaningful and deep has in some way become sick or twisted, a job that brought you satisfaction has become a ruler without mercy. If you have broken open that hornet's nest—ask for God's help, and don't stop there, reach out to others who can help you as well—a loved one, a priest, a counselor; who can help you find your way to hope.

A PRAYER

God, give me grace to accept with serenity
the things that cannot be changed,
Courage to change the things
which should be changed,
and the wisdom to distinguish
the one from the other.

Living one day at a time,
Enjoying one moment at a time,
Accepting hardship as a pathway to peace,
Taking, as Jesus did,
This sinful world as it is,
Not as I would have it,
Trusting that You will make all things right,
If I surrender to Your will,
So that I may be reasonably happy in this life,
And supremely happy with You forever in the next.
Amen.

— Reinhold Niebuhr, d. 1971[4]

---

4   Often known as the "Serenity Prayer," and used in portion or full by those in recovery groups and ministries.

Missing the Mark and Hitting the Bulls-eye

"...since all have sinned and fall short of the glory of God; they are now justified by his grace as a gift, through the redemption that is in Christ Jesus..."

— Romans 3:23-24

What do you do when you fall flat on your face?

It was a big day for me. Before supper, at camp, high scores and major achievements were announced to all gathered. As a young man, I was not much of an athlete, but on this day, I was top dog. The camp director announced that of the dozens of youth who had tried their hand at bow and arrow that day, my score outranked them all. In fact, I had even hit a bulls-eye at some fifty yards. Applause...applause. Then dinner. That was the high water mark of my archery career, and it was not repeated again—ever. On other evenings, other campers were recognized, but on most of those, I had missed the mark.

Some translations of the Bible use the word "sin" for the Greek word *hamartia*. *Hamartia* was an archery term which literally meant to *"miss the mark."* Missing the mark did not mean you were not trying to hit the bulls-eye, nor did it mean that you were even carelessly aiming; it meant that despite your efforts, you missed hitting dead center. With regard to sin, Paul tells the Roman Church, we all miss the mark—we are all, all of us, sinners.

That may seem like bad news, I suppose, but is it really? If we are all—I mean *all*—of us sinners, does that not also mean we are all in the same boat? If you feel yourself to be someone who has it "mostly right," maybe you feel a bit cheated, but then if you know your faults as you should, it should take away what might be a bit of envy for the more saintly. Whether sinner or saint, Paul says, we all fall short of the glory of God.

There are deeper matters at work, but the less complex way to put it is simply to say that only God is perfectly good, holy and righteous—only God. There are times, when we may hit dead center, but more often than not, we miss it. But that is not all Paul writes, is it?

The same ones who are all sinners, are also *"...now justified by His grace as a gift through the redemption that is in Christ Jesus..."* This means that though our aim is off; through our trust in Jesus, God straightens up the bow and as the match comes to an end, we are named winners every time.

This does not negate the times we have blown it; it means that when we have, we take our missed marks to the mercy and forgiveness of Jesus. We admit our aim is off—sometimes for reasons of our own choosing, sometimes not—either way, we admit that our final score is not worthy of being recognized in any way as a *"win."* When we do that—admit our sin—that is precisely what God wants us to do. And when we do, He meets us not with a medal for last place, but a trophy of grace and justification.

The apostle John would later write, *"If we confess our sins, he who is faithful and just will forgive us our sins and cleanse us from all unrighteousness."*[1] Good news, is it not? Confess...check. To the One who is faithful and just...check. Who then forgives us and cleanses us...check.

From all (not some, or even a lot, but all!) unrighteousness... check! **Bulls-eye!**

This is an important piece of one's Christian journey to understand as it is directly linked to your relationship with God. If you feel you are righteous without the help of Jesus Christ, then frankly, you will never see your need of

---

1   I John 1:9.

Him. If you feel beyond redemption, that there is no way you can ever be what God calls you to be, well then you will always, in some way, feel separated from Him. God does not want either—your self-righteousness or your self-separation. So He, God, chooses to justify things—to put them right.

Fredrick Buechner helps us here a bit;

> *"In printers' language to 'justify' means to set type in such a way that all full lines are of equal length and flush both left and right; in other words to put the printed lines in the right relationship with the page they're printed on and with each other. The religious sense of the word is very close to this. Being justified means being brought into right relation. Paul says simply that being justified means having peace with God (Romans 5:1). He uses the noun 'Justification' for the first step in the process of salvation.*
>
> *"...no matter what you've done, God wants you on His side. There is nothing you have to do or be. It's on the house. It goes with the territory. God has 'justified you,' lined you up. To feel this somehow in your bones is the first step on the way to being saved."[2]*

So if you are feeling on top of the world with your win today, remember that in all likelihood, you will miss the mark tomorrow; in fact, most of the time you will. At those times, remember you have a place to take those losses, you have someone to take them to—and He is willing to forgive, cleanse, and justify. I think that is one of the reasons we call our faith "The Good News."

---

2   Fredrick Buechner, *Wishful Thinking: A Theological ABC* (San Francisco: Harper & Row, 1973), 48–49.

Summer Time

Take a moment or two and consider some of your wins in life's journey. How long did the feeling of being a winner last? Think of some of your losses. How did you make your way beyond them? Now think of the times you missed the mark when it came to sin. Do you buy that we are all of us sinners? Is there good news in that for you? More importantly, do you believe that as all of us sin, all of us can also be justified through Jesus Christ? Is there a loss you need to take to Him today? He promises when you do, you will be forgiven and cleansed—the whole way through. Is there any reason to wait any longer?

A PRAYER

We thank You, O Father, for Your readiness to hear and to forgive; for Your great love to us, in spite of our unworthiness; for the many blessings we enjoy above our deserving, hoping, or asking. You have been so good to us in our ingratitude, thoughtlessness, and our forgetfulness of you. For Your pity, long-suffering, gentleness and tenderness, we bow our heads in humble and thankfulness of heart. We worship You Who are infinite love, infinite compassion, infinite power. Accept our praise and gratitude; through Jesus Christ our Lord and Savior. Amen.

— C. J. N. Child[3]

---

3   Batchelor, *The Doubleday Prayer Collection*, 34.

Everyone?

"The scripture says, 'No one who believes in him will be put to shame.' For there is no distinction between Jew and Greek; the same Lord is Lord of all and is generous to all who call on him. For, 'Everyone who calls on the name of the Lord shall be saved.'"

— Romans 10:11-13

....

How can you better love those whom you would rather not?

I was never big on what I will call "enforced play," particularly when it was enforced during my summer breaks. When I was a kid, I felt summer was for *me!* I had worked hard during the school year, and when school was "out for the summer," (a la *Alice Cooper* for those of you who remember the song) the days ahead belonged to *me*...except when they did not. When was that?

Visiting a relative only to be greeted by cousins I never knew, picking teams at summer camp, double dating with a couple with whom I did not want to double date, and so on. It is hard to connect with someone when you really have no interest in connecting—even harder to like them. And when they have a rotten personality, why bother?

It is even more difficult to get one's head around the fact that the God of our faith really calls on us to do our best to free ourselves of the task of judging another's relationship with God. This is one of the oldest and greatest challenges to authentic Christian expression. It seems part of our human nature to want to be right—and frankly to be the "most right" when it comes to the big questions.

There was a great deal going on in the Church in Rome—but much of it had to do with those choosing who was "in" and who was "out" when it came to being on God's team. You would have to read all of Romans (and all of the New Testament by the way) to get your head around the specifics. Some were saying only those who had become Jews before becoming Christians would be saved by God; others were saying you could bypass the Jewish faith altogether; while others fell somewhere in-between.

Paul cuts to the chase in the passage above. He points them back to Isaiah, recalling for his readers that God does not show favoritism when it comes to those who call out to Him.[1] He then goes on to just put it out there—*"Everyone who calls on the name of the Lord will be saved."* Come on, *everyone? Really?*

Much of the violent conflict in our world today is not so much over issues of politics as it is over issues of religion. I am a Christian because I do believe what the Scriptures of the Old and New Testament teach us about the best way to be in a relationship with God—through submission to Jesus Christ as Lord and Savior, and living day-to-day with the aid and power of God's Holy Spirit; a commitment and decision I have made—a way of life I have chosen to live. When I have the opportunity to tell others about the Christian faith, even those of other faiths, I do so; but here is the rub, in order to be a Christian, I do not (nor should I) have to suspend a belief that everyone who has experienced a relationship with God has to do it *my way*.

Paul's injunction here puts us on guard against judging not just other Christians, but those of other faiths, or those of no faith. In his landmark argument for the Christian Faith, *The Case for Christianity*, C.S. Lewis proposes a merciful approach for Christians tempted to not want to play well with others;

> *"I am going to begin by telling you one thing that Christians don't need to believe. If you are a Christian you don't have to believe that all the other religions are simply wrong all through.... If you are a Christian, you are free to think that all these religions, even the queerest ones, contain at least some hint of the truth. When I was an atheist I had to try to persuade myself that the whole human race were pretty good fools until about one hundred years ago; when I became a Christian I was able to take a more liberal view. But, of course, being a Christian does mean thinking*

1   See Isaiah 8:14; 28:16 and Romans 9:33.

113

that where Christianity differs from other religions, Christianity is right and they are wrong. Like in arithmetic—there's only one right answer to a sum, and all other answers are wrong: but some of the wrong answers are much nearer being right than others."[2]

Now both Lewis and Paul would agree on two things. The first is that there is a necessity for one who calls him or herself a Christian, and one who seeks to be in a saving relationship with God, to call on the Lord. But they would also agree that when it comes to "how" one calls on the Lord, the prescription may be a good bit more loose than the human heart and psyche could ever conceive or understand.

I spend a good bit of my life guiding people toward a personal faith in Christ, helping them (within my own meager means) to better understand the teachings of our faith and moving them toward our sacred sacramental acts—baptism, confirmation, the Lord's Supper. These are all gifts to humankind to get to know God better, but much like the laws God gives to us, they are meant to serve God's children, not the other way 'round.[3]

Do you remember the thief on the cross? Crucified next to Jesus, he was honest enough to confess that while he was deserving of his sentence, Jesus was not. We know very little about the thief. We can assume at least some things based on what we do not know—the man

might have known of Jesus but was probably not a follower, he was not baptized or confirmed, he had not been to church or experienced a First Communion class, he had not come forward when invited by an itinerant preacher to make a public confession of faith. We know this—he was a sinner, a condemned man, crucified alongside Jesus, and had the humility to utter nine words that would change his fate,

2   C. S. Lewis, *The Case for Christianity* (New York: MacMillan Company, 1948), 31. (Note: this portion would later be included in various versions of Lewis' *Mere Christianity*.)
3   See Meditation 26 in this book.

"Jesus, remember me when you come into your kingdom."[4] Jesus' reply? *"Truly I tell you, today you will be with me in Paradise."*[5]

Let me circle back to where I began. I opened this little meditation saying that when I was a kid, I did not much like being "forced" to play with those I did not much like. That kind of thinking could easily move me to simply write another person off altogether. If I am honest, my tendency against enforced play did not go away when I reached the adult years. Exclusion of the "other" for whatever reason, particularly if it taints my understanding of God and His mercy, is foolhardy.

I admit, sometimes it is hard to swallow Paul's words, *"Everyone who calls on the name of the Lord,"* particularly if I perceive they are playing for a team not my own. But then, that is not my call to make, is it?

 ### Summer Time

Think of someone whom you think might never make their way into the circle of God's mercy. Perhaps it is the name of someone in particular; or just a group—political, religious, a persuasion, a lifestyle. Think on Paul's words. Think on Lewis' words. Think on Jesus' words to that thief on the Cross. How can you better love the one you would rather not? Specifically, how?

A PRAYER

O God, you have made of one blood all the peoples of the earth, and sent your blessed Son to preach peace to those who are far off and to those who are near: Grant that people everywhere may seek after you and find you; bring the nations into your fold; pour out your Spirit upon all flesh; and hasten the coming of your kingdom; through Jesus Christ our Lord. Amen.

— The Book of Common Prayer[6]

---

4   Luke 23:42.
5   Luke 23:43.
6   *The Book of Common Prayer*, 1979, 100.

Have Love

"If I speak in the tongues of mortals and of angels, but do not have love, I am a noisy gong or a clanging cymbal. And if I have prophetic powers, and understand all mysteries and all knowledge, and if I have all faith, so as to remove mountains, but do not have love, I am nothing. If I give away all my possessions, and if I hand over my body so that I may boast, but do not have love, I gain nothing....the greatest of these is love...."

— I Corinthians 13:1-3, 13

What is love to you?

It is a hot August day in Houston as I write this meditation. This morning, I put my eighteen-year-old son on a plane to head toward his freshman year at college. I imagine we were both thinking lots of things, and most of his had to do with the future—a freshman year, new friends, a new city, a new adventure. My thoughts had mostly to do with the past, memories shared, from infancy to late teens—having him in the house, what I will miss without him here.

Relationships are treasures God entrusts to us. Some last for brief seasons, some for a lifetime, but few, if any of them, have depth, meaning, and substance without love—authentic, self-giving love. It would have meant very little to my boy today if I said, "Before you leave, I want you to remember all the clothes and meals your mother and I provided for you, the homes and utilities that made you comfortable, your toys, your vacations." That would have meant very little in a moment that really is just worthy of a good hug and three solid words, "I love you."

Love is an emotion we feel, but more often than not, it is a decision we make—to bless the life of another by giving ourselves to them. Paul teaches us in this famous "Love Chapter" that is so often read at wedding services, that duty done for the sake of duty is just duty, but buoyed with love—duty becomes selfless gift.

My parents took us on a number of great vacations over the years. For a season, my father was a single parent raising three kids. One year we had spent several weeks preparing for our annual trip to the beach, several days packing, ending with a long day driving. We had just settled into our hotel room when I developed an earache. At first, I tried to brush it off, but it got worse and when I told my father, he immediately sprang into action. First medicine, constant "check-ins," and finally a call to the doc back home. When dull turned to excruciating, he made the decision to pack the car up and take us back home. Um, I was not hero to my two sisters, but I think my father became even more of a hero to me.

He could have easily gotten angry and told me to buck up. I suppose he could have ignored the whole thing. He could have pointed to all the planning and preparation that had gone into finding a nice place to stay on a beautiful beach with adventures a plenty and meals on the ready—but you know, without love, those things mean very little. All of that, frankly, meant nothing compared to a father's concern, care, and love for a son.

I will confess, love does not always come easy—even when we love another. Our self-ward tendencies as human beings keep us from that key ingredient in the decision of love—self-giving. So the only real way to grow in the motivation, the power, and the expression of love is to be connected to the Author of love. *"God is love..."* the apostle John tells his reader.[1] But we know that, do we not? Really, we know deep down that love comes as a gift—a divine gift. As we

---

1   I John 4:8.

are connected to God, we are connected to love; and as to love, to the other that God gives into our lives.

Love heals our selfish motives in caring for others. Peter, writing to the infant Christian community of his day, reminded them *"Above all, maintain a constant love for one another, for love covers a multitude of sins."*[2] And when we are tempted to think there is something of the Christian faith that matters more than love, there is Paul once again to kick us in line—*"the only thing that counts is faith working through love."*[3] The *only* thing.

Authentic love is really hard to describe, but Paul hits as close as possible the proverbial nail on the head with this love chapter. His entry as to what love is not (actions without love) steps further by describing what it is—not envious or boastful, arrogant or rude, not irritable or resentful...it bears all things, believes all things, hopes all things, endures all things; it never ends—love lasts.[4] As Shakespeare would write, *"Love is not love which alters when it alteration finds, or bends with the remover to remove. O, no, it is an ever-fixed mark, that looks on tempests and is never shaken...."*[5] And when I am tempted to stray from the decision to love or when I am strained or feel too weak to love, I need only return to the Source of that Love, who loves me with a perfect love so that I can, even with all my human frailty, love more as He does, in a way that lasts.

I remember lots of vacations with my parents, but maybe the one I remember most is the one when love bypassed the plans. I hope my son remembers all the things we did and places we went over the last eighteen years leading up to this morning when I said goodbye and let him go, but they would not mean much at all if I did not love him. That, I hope he remembers.

Really, the only thing that counts is to have love.

---

2   I Peter 4:8.
3   Galatians 5:6.
4   I Corinthians 13:4–8.
5   From Sonnet 116.

Summer Time

Who needs your love this day? Who needs you to love as God loves you? Can you choose to love that one without limits, without "if onlys" or "whens"—just now, today, as he or she is; as they are? For that one who so needs it from you—can you have love?

A Prayer

O God, in whom nothing can live but as it lives in love, grant us the spirit of love which does not want to be rewarded, honoured or esteemed, but only to become the blessing and happiness of everything that wants it; love which is the very joy of life, and thine own goodness and truth within the soul; who thyself art love, and by love our redeemer, from eternity to eternity.

— William Law, d. 1761

Be Reconciled

*"...if anyone is in Christ, there is a new creation: everything
old has passed away; see, everything has become new! All
this is from God, who reconciled us to Himself through
Christ, and has given us the ministry of reconciliation; that
is, in Christ God was reconciling the world to himself, not
counting their trespasses against them, and entrusting the
message of reconciliation to us. So we are ambassadors
for Christ, since God is making His appeal through us; we
entreat you on behalf of Christ, be reconciled to God."*

— II Corinthians 5:17-20

Are you reconciled to God?

As a younger man, I did a good bit of whitewater rafting. One of
the most challenging rivers was the Chattooga, where the movie
Deliverance was filmed. Our journey began in South Carolina and
ended just south of the Georgia border. The river was filled with
currents slow and raging and some of the most intense rapids were
strenuously exhilarating to say the least (or perhaps exhilaratingly
strenuous!). Fortunately, we had an expert guide along the way.

There was only one rapid that required a special stop. Our guide
told us to paddle to shore and get out. A short hike put us over this
particular rapid that had several jagged rocks and two steep drop-offs.
He explained to us that this series of rapids ranged between Class IV
and Class V.[1] He told us we had the option of getting out then and

---

1   A Class V is the most treacherous level of a river current, and carried the threat of great harm
     or even death.

meeting up downriver with whomever decided to go through the rapids. He made no bones about it—it would be a wild ride, and could be a dangerous ride, if we did not follow his directions to a tee.

What our guide was doing was giving us all an opportunity to reconcile ourselves to what that rapid would surely deliver. We did not have to go through if we did not want to do so. But we could not, if we were not (deep down) willing to take the plunge, if you will.

The Church in Corinth proved to be one of Paul's wildest rides. It was a large port city, and like most port cities that often served as cultural crossroads in the ancient world, it was a fishbowl of virtually every race, ethnicity, religion and persuasion. Preaching the Gospel there was a huge challenge, and even after those who received Paul's message came to faith, keeping them together—unified, reconciled to God and one another—proved an ongoing challenge. There were constant divisions in the Corinthian Church, and Paul spent a great deal of the Corinthian correspondence steering these early Christians back to a safe shore.[2]

In the passage above, Paul lifts up what he calls a *"ministry of reconciliation."* We know from other passages in the Corinthian

---

2   What we know to be I and II Corinthians was likely pieces of at least four letters, one of which appears to be missing, but all of them deal pretty squarely with the divisions.

correspondence that loving one another was key—was essential—to being a faithful Christian.[3] In this passage, he reminds them of the source for reconciliation—God, who chose to reconcile Himself to humankind, who chose, despite our sinful ways, to press on in His journey to reconcile Himself, through Christ, to all who would receive Him.

Paul uses this mini-essay to implore his audience to be reconciled. He, like our little river guide, makes it clear—God chose to go through the rapids first. God looked ahead and saw the painful, dangerous, and ultimately deadly journey that would be required to reconcile humankind to Himself. Reconciliation, for God, would not come without cost.

Now, as we have already considered, reconciliation is a gift to us from God, one that comes without our paying the cost. The cost, if you will, comes after we receive God's reconciliation. The cost is the price of being a disciple—inviting Christ into our lives, receiving  His Spirit, and relinquishing our control such that He can make all things new. As Paul points out, *"if anyone is in Christ, there is a new creation: everything old has passed away, everything has become new!"*

Notice that exclamation point—Paul did not use them often. This was a big announcement—reconciliation with God brought but one cost to the follower—a new beginning. Jesus said it would be like a new birth.[4]

One of the many good things about our faith is that it does not hide much. It tells truths in simple and enduring ways—God loves us; God seeks to be reconciled to us; God sent His Son not to condemn us but to save us; and if we would but believe, we would have new life altogether.[5]

---

3   See Meditation 33 in this book.
4   See John 3:1–21.
5   Specifically, John 3:16–17.

New life can be scary at times, but when the old life has worn out its welcome, it really is the only way forward. Paul reminds us the journey to that new life is to be reconciled to God. The good news is that He has done all the work; your only choice is whether or not to go along for the ride.

By the way, I did decide to reconcile myself to go through that rapid. I held fast to every word spoken by our guide, and when we made it to the other side, I felt like a new man altogether.

 Summer Time

Let us pause now, well into our summer meditations and consider a really important question—are you reconciled to God in Christ? The whole of our faith is about holding fast to the mercy and love of Christ Himself, but in order to hold fast to Him, you have to let go of anything else that might get in the way of this reconciliation. Imagine Christ pulling you ashore from your daily life and taking you up on a hill to look down at the life you now live. Is there anything, anyone, you might need to release so that you can be united to Him? Reconciled to Him? Name it...give yourself into the hands of our Divine Guide. He will get you to the other side and you will be, well, born anew.

A Prayer

Be born in us,
Incarnate Love.
take our flesh and blood,
and give us Your humanity;
take our eyes, and give us your vision;
take our minds,
and give us Your pure thought;
take our feet and set them in your path;
take our hands and fold them in Your prayer;
take our hearts
and give them Your will to love....

Nail our hands
in Your hands
to the Cross.
make us take and hold
the hard thing.
Nail our feet,
in Your feet
to the Cross,
that they may never
wander away from You.
Make our promises and our vows,
nails that hold us fast,
that even the dead weight of sin,
dragging on the nails
In our last weakness,
may not separate us from You,
but may make us one with You
in Your redeeming love.
Amen.

— Frances Caryll Houselander, d. 1954[6]

---

6   Maisie Ward, *The Splendor of the Rosary* (London: Sheed and Ward, 1945).

What Do You Do With the Thorns?

"....so that no one may think better of me than what is seen in me or heard from me, even considering the exceptional character of the revelations. Therefore, to keep me from being too elated, a thorn was given me in the flesh, a messenger of Satan to torment me, to keep me from being too elated. Three times I appealed to the Lord about this, that it would leave me, but he said to me, 'My grace is sufficient for you, for power is made perfect in weakness.' So, I will boast all the more gladly of my weaknesses, so that the power of Christ may dwell in me."

— II Corinthians 12:6-9

"See what large letters I make when I am writing in my own hand!"

— Galatians 6:11

What do you do with your thorns?

A black skimmer is a tern-like sea bird that lives along the coasts of southern North America and northern South America. One of the reasons for its name is that it gathers its food by flying very low, right over the top of the water, then opening its lower mandible and "skimming" its prey from the water's surface. Ornithologists have noticed an interesting fact about these birds: if taken away from the water, and if not allowed to skim, the lower mandible will grow beyond its usefulness. The resistance of the water against its

125

lower beak during the skimming actually wears it down such that it becomes more the creature God created it to be. To keep it from this resistance, this wearing down, actually retards nature's way.

I became fascinated with skimmers when I honed in on a favorite (and secret!) fishing spot near a jetty along the Gulf Coast of Florida. Whether early in the morning or late in the afternoon, the spot I picked was also a favorite of several of these interesting birds. As I fished, I would watch as they did. I would return to this spot year after year, learning from them, meditating on this unique process, and coming to the conclusion that for whatever reason, God allows for struggle to be part of the drama of existence.

Paul wrote to the Corinthians of a "thorn" given to him—something that tormented him and that he had asked God to remove three different times. Most scholars believe it might have well been poor eyesight, the result of his catching malaria during an earlier missionary journey. It was Paul's practice to dictate his letters, in all likelihood due to this thorn. We see at the end of his letter to the Galatians, that he has taken the writing instrument from his secretary to write in his own hand with *"large letters,"* because, no doubt, such large letters were necessary when writing with poor vision, but, as those who knew Paul also knew he had poor eyesight, they were also proof that the one writing was Paul.

What are your thorns? You may have a physical ailment, or it may be mental or emotional. You may be a poor athlete but an excellent student, or perhaps extraordinary athlete of average wit. Some of us get ill and never fully recover (think of stroke victims who partially recover, but are left with a limp or loss of speech).

Paul wanted to be rid of his thorns, but God said no. He said no, Paul says, because it was part of who God wanted Paul to be and, as Paul notes, it allowed the power of Christ to be made known more through what he perceived was his own deficiency.

I do not think I fully understood all of this until I met my friend Emily during my days as a university chaplain. Emily suffered a bout with rheumatic fever as an infant, and as a fruit of that sickness her body was racked with rheumatoid arthritis. By the time we met, she had undergone a dozen surgeries; her limbs were (from my perspective) stunted from their full growth potential. She needed help carrying a lunch tray or walking up stairs—something which most of us take for granted.

I do not think I ever saw Emily without a smile or good word for another. She was deeply committed to her faith, and I confess I often pondered what I perceived as the "unfairness" of her challenge. I once asked her if she could change anything about her life, what would it be. After a pause, she said, "Nothing. I would not change a thing. This disability has demanded that I lean on Christ more and more every single day. I have had to turn to Him every day and He has become my friend and companion that has enabled me to live with these scars." Emily went on to study theology. She later married and was ordained and is now a practicing priest. Indeed, she showed me how Christ's power can be made perfect in one's weakness. I would later read Helen Keller's words that remind me of Emily's faith; "We could never learn to be brave and patient if there were only joy in the world."

I guess God could have made an easier way for those skimmers to gobble down their meals, but then they would not be skimmers, would they? God could have removed Paul's thorn, but then Paul would not really be Paul, would he? God could have healed Emily in the wink of an eye, but then others would not have seen the power of Christ in her life, would they?

So, what do you do with your thorns?

Summer Time

Spiritualist Anthony de Mello wrote "Every painful event contains in itself a seed of growth and liberation." We can let thorns define us; or we can invite God into our thorns and then let them refine us. Define or refine. Which would you choose? What thorn do you face this day that you need to take to Christ, such that His liberating power can be more known through you?

A Prayer

Dear Jesus, who knew both despair and joy;
acquainted with grief, tears and pain,
but also with laughter, hope and health;

Come to my aid, please come to my places of brokenness;
walk through the weaknesses of my body, my mind, my heart, my soul,
as you might journey through a desert, and with each step you take,
refresh and renew my parched and empty spaces.

Where healing I desire accords not with Your perfect will,
help me to accept my thorns, not as a measure of my own worth;
but as Your gift so that You may be known even more powerfully through them.

As you stepped from hell and death,
into life and resurrection;
So resurrect hells and deaths of my own making, and that of others;
that I may know You to be the best Way, the only Truth,
and the most perfect Life.
Amen.

No Difference

"...for in Christ Jesus you are all children of God through faith. As many of you as were baptized into Christ have clothed yourselves with Christ. There is no longer Jew or Greek, there is no longer slave or free, there is no longer male and female; for all of you are one in Christ Jesus. And if you belong to Christ, then you are Abraham's offspring, heirs according to the promise."

— Galatians 3:26–29

Do you need the gift of colorblindness?

I mentioned earlier that I am an aquarium buff. When setting up a saltwater aquarium, an experienced hobbyist is not just filling up the tank; he or she will try and set up a balanced ecosystem. Once the balance is achieved, with the exception of regular cleaning, the tanks are pretty simple to maintain.

Achieving that balance has to do with several things, however— proper chemicals, substrate, live rock, coral and, frankly, species that have enough space and time to learn to live with one another. This season of preparation is called "acclimation." If done correctly, before long you can witness a small miracle of nature as invertebrates and fish of all colors, sizes, temperaments, and textures live together in harmony.

It does not always work that way—sometimes inbred aggression or territorial protection invades a community—and it is usually not a pretty sight! But that is nature's way.

However, when it comes to God's community, that is not God's way. The Church in Galatia was, as were so many other early Christian communities it seems, divided in many ways. One of the major divisions was between Jews who had become Christians and Christians

129

who had bypassed the Jewish faith and found faith in Jesus without the grounding of Hebrew forebears. The questions of who was to be in and who was to be out, who was greater and who was lesser, were almost a constant irritant to the Galatian Christian ecosystem.

Paul took a shot at putting the argument to death, *"in Christ, there are no differences...you are all children of faith...you all belong to Christ..."* Enough said? One would hope so, but humans, it seems, have an almost natural tendency to divide ourselves over color, ethnicity, gender, sexual orientation, faith—even geography! In its least offensive forms it is unfortunate and at times downright silly, but at its worst it rears an ugly head and wears names like discrimination, prejudice, racism.

It doesn't take a rocket scientist to figure out I have a Jewish name. My great grandfather came to this country at the turn of the last century, fleeing the pogroms of old Russia. His son, my grandfather, married the daughter of a Baptist minister, and that was the end of that!

I grew up in Birmingham, Alabama, during the 1960s, and it was not uncommon for classmates to call me a "Jew-boy," and suggest at times that, despite the fact that I had grown up a Christian, I should sit with the "other Jews" who either by choice or coercion tended to segregate themselves at lunch hour and on the playground. I found ways to laugh and shrug it off, but I knew I lived in a city where much worse than name-calling was carried out with fire hoses, attack dogs, lynchings, and even bombings. Many of these horrific acts were carried out by supposedly well-meaning, churchgoing Christians. It is an embarrassment of which all humans should be ashamed.

I have been fortunate to travel much of my nation and to other nations as well, and I found that what one could find in Birmingham in the 1960s was not limited to the south; it could easily be found (in different ways) in the north, east, and west. Discrimination projected from white to black, could also be found from black to white. In Mexico, it was made plain to me by an Aztec South American that some believed Mayans were to be treated differently. I heard the same thing when I learned that animosity sometimes exists between Japanese and Koreans. And so it goes, and as it does, so much pain is wrought—a tear in the fabric of Jesus' intended ecosystem.

I suppose one gift I have been given is that I am a smorgasbord of the human gene pool. I carry blood from ancestors who were Irish, Scottish, English, Russian, Hebrew, German and even Creek Indian. I suspect there is more in there as well. This I know, Paul's words enjoin us to plead for a gift of colorblindness.

By colorblindness I am not suggesting we ignore our differences,

our individual uniqueness (which is, of course, a gift of God) but I am suggesting that we ask for hearts that embrace all as if they were the same, love all as if there was no difference whatsoever. That kind of colorblindness is—make no mistake—a Christian virtue that we are all called to receive.

Frederich Buechner pokes us a bit here when he writes,

> "When Jesus said to love your neighbor, a lawyer who was present asked him to clarify what he meant by neighbor. He wanted a legal definition he could refer to in case the question of loving one ever happened to come up....

> "Instead Jesus told the story of the Good Samaritan, the point of which seems to be that your neighbor is to be construed as meaning anybody who needs you. The lawyer's response is left unrecorded."[1]

My grandfather opened and operated a retail store just a few blocks from the 16th Street Baptist Church, where four little girls were killed by a bomb blast as they sat in a room in Jesus' house of worship, on Sunday, September 15, 1963. One of his chief mottos for his business was, *"Folks is just folks...everyone is to be treated the same way, no matter who they are."* It was his own private way of saying no to a horror that filled the streets near his workplace. It was his way of being colorblind. It was a business practice I observed throughout my childhood, and it, along with my growing Christian faith, was a good teacher whenever my more biased human tendencies would get the best of me.

---

1   Buechner, *Wishful Thinking*, 65-66.

No one is sure who wrote this little verse, but it is worth putting to memory;

> *"Hated, despised a thing to flout;*
> *They drew a circle that left me out.*
> *But love and I had the wit to win;*
> *We drew a circle that took them in."*
> *"In Christ, there is no difference...**no** difference."*

 ## Summer Time

It is fair to say that no one is innocent of some form of disdain of others for some reason not born of their own character, but of their very nature. Summer slowness offers a good opportunity to really consider whether you are colorblind. If you visit the beach or a camping area, a theater, or amusement park, you will likely see people of every shape, size, color, and variety. When those differences draw out of you a thought of heart or mind, can you ask God to strike you blind? Strike you...colorblind?

A Prayer

O God, you have made of one blood all the peoples of the earth, and sent your blessed Son to preach peace to those who are far off and to those who are near; Grant that people everywhere may seek after you and find you; bring the nations into your fold; pour out your Spirit upon all flesh; and hasten the coming of your kingdom; through Jesus Christ our Lord. Amen.

— The Book of Common Prayer[2]

---

2 *The Book of Common Prayer*, 1979, 100.

Imitation of a Life

*"Therefore be imitators of God, as beloved children, and
live in love, as Christ loved us and gave himself up for us, a
fragrant offering and sacrifice to God."*

— Ephesians 5:1-2

How might Christ be calling on you to imitate Him?[1]

Some years ago now, someone reminded us to ask how we might
imitate Christ by producing bracelets, T-shirts, bumper stickers and
note cards with four simple letters—"WWJD?"prompting the question
to ask "What would Jesus do?" It was hard to go a day or two without
seeing the letters in some version, some color, some script. It was a
good question, and a very popular trend while it lasted, and our Lord
certainly got some great publicity.

The idea behind the WWJD campaign was simple: what if we really
responded to every situation by asking ourselves that question?
What would Jesus do in this traffic jam? What would Jesus say to our
naughty child? Would Jesus go see that movie? Would Jesus judge
that person as I have? Would I forgive as Jesus does? The main point
was that we need to be more in the mind of Christ, and attempting
to be more like Him. We need to be imitators of Christ in every aspect
of our lives.

It is hard to be like Jesus—in part, well, because we are not Him! But it
begs the question—why is this so hard? Why do we do the things we
ought not to do, and not do the things we ought? We were created in
the likeness of Christ, He lives in our hearts, but His perfection seems
to constantly elude us.

---

1   This meditation was written by Laura Levenson.

When I am sitting in the pew on Sunday, listening to the choir and basking in the loveliness of my surroundings, I am so inspired to take that feeling into the rest of my week. Every week I pray that the peace and love I feel for everyone around me would remain permanently and never waver. Then I leave church, the reality of life hits, and I am a simple, flawed human again. How disappointing!

When Paul wrote the Christians in Ephesus, he had a great deal to say, but perhaps few words more poignant than *"Be imitators of God."* It was almost as if Paul was saying, in his own Pauline way, "WWJD?" But it is one thing to suggest it, another to ask it and another still to live it! I may know what Jesus would do, and not want to do it! But I know deep down, when I fail to imitate Him in thought, or word, or deed, I am treading on dangerous ground.

It is almost as if I need a trail guide. I have been on a number of hikes and I always seemed to get more out of them when I paid close attention to the guide or Scout leader; sometimes if I did not, I would get sidetracked, and could even potentially lose my way. I have often thought of Jesus in this way. He is the perfect trail guide. If I want get the most out of life, I need to follow in His footsteps, listen to the things He says, watch where He points, and step over and around the dangerous places He clearly avoids. This sometimes means I do not always get to go where I want.

As a born introvert, I have had to live the life of an extrovert. For many years I felt as though I had a foot in two worlds, each one tending to threaten the existence of the other. The hostess, board

member, Sunday School teacher, and so on, yearned to be in the solitude of her garden. The quiet gardener, after a while, missed the company and fellowship of the world outside. Only after years of walking with God did I understand that He needed me to be both. The path I would have chosen would never have been as fulfilling or as interesting as the one God had in mind.

God's call on our lives sometimes leads us on unexpected paths toward unexpected roles. We seek His will for our lives, and we trust Him to guide our steps, and watch with wonder as the path takes mysterious turns and twists. Just like wandering down an unknown trail in the mountains, we can't always see and know what is just around the bend. Over the next crest could be a beautiful wildflower...or a snake! Muddy tree roots reach up to trip us. Poison ivy wafts at our ankles. A lovely cool stream offers refreshing water. Every step brings us closer to a new revelation.

While hiking a mountain trail a few years ago, we were reminded how important guides can be. As we followed our simple map on our eight-mile sojourn up the mountain, we were confident that we were doing just fine. We found ourselves enjoying the view so much

that we unknowingly wandered off our path. Our tranquil, peaceful walk suddenly became a search for our location. "This map is wrong," I remember hearing (or saying). We found ourselves at the top of the mountain with a wall of dense fog rolling toward us. The world around us became more and more hazy, and our cell phones had little reception. Alarmed, we prayed aloud as we searched for some guide to lead us back to our trail. Finally, we stumbled upon a fence, which we followed downhill, and which led us to the road, and back to a cabin where a comfortable fire and warm beverage were waiting for us.

How happy we were to be "home!" Those moments of confusion and loss were so very frightening! It was never the plan to become lost. It never is, is it?

Talking to God allows Him to give us His roadmap. It leads us away from confusion and doubt. Following him faithfully reveals His plan for our lives. Stopping for directions with the letters "WWJD" often is the best way to travel through life. In imitating Christ, we know we will always find the right way—which is so much better than our own!

Summer Time

What if you really allowed God to be your trail guide? Wouldn't He guide you home? Won't you take his hand?

A Prayer

Guide me, O Thou great Jehovah,
Pilgrim through this barren land.
I am weak, but Thou art mighty;
Hold me with Thy powerful hand.
Bread of Heaven, Bread of Heaven,
Feed me till I want no more;
Feed me till I want no more.
Amen.

— William Williams, d. 1791[2]

---

2   From the hymn "Guide Me O Thou Great Jehovah," 1762.

Press On

"I want to know Christ and the power of his resurrection...
Not that I have already obtained this or have already reached
the goal; but I press on to make it my own, because Christ
Jesus has made me his own. Beloved, I do not consider that
I have made it my own; but this one thing I do: forgetting
what lies behind and straining forward to what lies ahead, I
press on toward the goal for the prize of the heavenly call of
God in Christ Jesus...."

— Philippians 3:10a, 12-14

Is there anything preventing you from living fully into your relationship with our Lord?

I have been fortunate to have had several mentors over the years. My father has been a mentor, several clergy and professors, my wife—even all three of my children have been mentors to me. Relationship between a mentor and mentee must be mutual; it is a willingness on behalf of one to give to another. A good mentor will not give up on his or her mentee when they falter in receiving, and living into, the counsel offered—a good mentor will encourage his or her student to press on toward the goal—whatever that goal may be.

John Stott was an Anglican priest, teacher, theologian, and writer—and he was my friend and my mentor. We met decades ago during my first year of seminary. We stayed in touch and while we would visit on the U.S. side of the great pond, our more treasured visits were on his side in the United Kingdom. There we shared meals, conversations, prayer.[1]

---

1   Many will know that John Stott chose the bachelor's life of a worldwide evangelist, teacher, and mentor to hundreds, over the life of a husband. He felt as though he could only do one or the other, and could not do both well at the same time. Because of his choice, countless numbers of men and women knew him as "Uncle John," as did I.

As we both grew older, it got harder to get together. My duties as a parish priest with a growing family increased, and John's age and ability to easily travel began to wane. We had to press on in our relationship. But as I noted above, this good mentor always, **always** had an encouraging word—to persist in prayer, in the living out of my faith, to avoid the squabbles that so persistently seem to plague the church and its clergy and to be faithful to what I had been called to do—remembering always that I was not alone.

Our last visit was perhaps my most memorable. By now, John was in a retirement home for clergy at the last stop on a train out of central

London. He had invited me to come at the end of the day, but because of his failing health, he could not give more than an hour.

The journey to him was not really an easy one. I was the only one to get off at this particular station and it was well after dark. There were no signs pointing the way. I walked to the only nearby building with lights, a garage, and asked a mechanic if he knew where the retirement home was—"Down that road..." he pointed. There were no lights on that gravel path into the woods. I pressed on.

Eventually the path opened into a small gathering of buildings. Before long, I was ushered to John's room. He could not stand, but greeted me with a smile and embrace. We talked for a long time, but really it seemed not long enough. He encouraged me in so many ways to press on. We prayed together, hugged, and that was our last visit together before his death in July of 2011.

That last visit was a good metaphor for our relationship. To keep that relationship going, we had to press on. The time, the distance, the years—all would have been good reasons to throw in the towel, but then I would have missed his pervasive rally cry to press on.

You no doubt have a mentor, perhaps several, like John. Some will encourage you to press on in your roles—your job, your relationships. Paul was a mentor to his young protégé Timothy, with whom he wrote a letter to the Christians in Philippi. Perhaps in no other letter does Paul speak more plainly as an encouraging mentor, and his encouragement is to press on in their faith.

As we head toward the end of this collection of meditations, we have hopefully had increasing time to consider the many ways God relates to us, the ways we relate to God, and all to one another. But honesty presses us to admit that being a Christian is not always easy, and being faithful is often abhorrently difficult. Disappointment with others' failing and our own can be a scourge that makes our faith seem impotent in the face the tidal wave of challenges. To that wave, Paul says, *"Press on."*

Paul himself had seen, and would see even more, so many challenges to his faith, but he did not cut himself lose of the moorings of that faith, because he knew he was not alone. He had met a Companion in the Son of God, Jesus, and that same Jesus would not only see Paul through to the end, but then greeting him when the end came— having attained *"the goal for the prize of the heavenly call."*

Let us really, now, hone in on anything that might be diverting or even blocking a pure and unfettered relationship with Jesus Christ, be it fear or sin, shame or doubt, confusion or hopelessness—all can be vanquished if we can but receive the encouragement of Christ to press on.

It is said that perhaps one of Winston Churchill's most famous speeches was his commencement address at London's Harrow Hall in 1941. Having already seen challenges to his own leadership and no doubt to his faith in the face of a growing worldwide conflict, the peak of his speech was to the point, *"Never give in. Never give in. Never, never, never, never—in nothing, great or small, large or petty—never give in, except to convictions of honor and good sense."*

If your faith is challenged this day, or in the days to come, why not let Paul be your mentor? Whatever it takes, go the distance; do not be discouraged; do not give way to despair. Another of my mentors, John Claypool used to tell me, *"Despair is presumptuous, as it whispers that God has relinquished His power to transform."* To such despair, Paul would whisper back—"Press on." Worth a try, do you not think?

Summer Time

What is it that narrows your spiritual arteries such that the heart is strained from knowing the love and hope of God in Christ Jesus? Name it, now. Write it down here if you wish. Then give it to the One who can, and will, transform it into something you cannot now imagine. For the love of God—literally—press on.

A Prayer

Nada te turbe,
Nada te espante.
Toda se pasa.
Dios no se muda.
La paciencia todo lo alcanza.
Quien a Dios tiene nada le falta.

Solos Dios basta.

Let nothing disturb you,
Nothing dismay you.
All things pass.
God never changes.
Patience obtains all things.
Whoever has God lacks nothing,
God is enough.

— Teresa of Avila, d. 1582

Serious Business

"Rejoice in the Lord always; again I will say, Rejoice."

— Philippians 4:4

Can you give way to joy?

When was your last good, deep-down moment of joy? In the preface, I recalled C.S. Lewis' teaching that moments when we seem to let our self go—dance, laughter, frivolity, seemed somehow *"out of place"* here in our day-to-day lives, because, as Lewis suggested, this is not their regular place, they are but a moment's escape—*summer time* if you will—from the lives you and I were put here to live.

I do not know about you, but I find my greatest moments of joy as moments when I have lost myself into something else completely. Sometimes that happens on vacation with my loved ones, perhaps at a concert or good movie, other times after a great meal or in the arms of my wife. When one finds joy in these kinds of moments, what is happening is that the self is lost, and is giving way to something or someone else.

Paul found pure joy in giving Himself to Jesus Christ. Philippians is often called the "joyful letter" because Paul uses some form of the word *joy* more in this one letter than he does in all the other letters of his we have, combined. And yet, some might think this strange, because Paul wrote this particular letter from prison around the year 60 A.D.

141

In the previous few years, this committed apostle had been whipped, beaten, and rejected by his own friends and religious community. As he wrote these words, "rejoice," he faced a verdict on his life. Eventually, Paul's judges would sentence him to beheading during the persecution of Nero. Yet in the midst of all this, facing all that was to come, Paul was not angry or bitter. No, he said "Rejoice." "Rejoice."

Why? If we read on, we see Paul unpacking this a bit more:

> *"I know what it is to have little, and I know what it is to have plenty. In any and all circumstances I have learned the secret of being well-fed and of going hungry, of having plenty and being in need. I can do all things through him who strengthens me."*[1]

Paul found the source of his joy to be Christ. The witness of our faith testifies that the surest path to real joy is to give one's life to Christ. Leon Bloy once wrote *"Joy is the most infallible sign of the presence of God."* Samuel Moor Shoemaker wrote, *"The surest mark of a Christian is not faith, or even love, but joy."* Mother Teresa was fond of saying *"A joyful heart is the normal result of a heart burning with love."* And E. Stanley Jones confessed, *"When I met Christ, I felt that I had swallowed sunshine!"*

We should not confuse joy with giddiness or even happiness, as these are temporary conditions. One can slip from happiness into sadness in a moment's notice. But joy—joy transcends such temporary satisfactions.

Being joyful does not always mean one has a smile on face and in heart...but joy is a light quality that is the fruit of a faithful, committed, ongoing relationship with the One who is bigger than the world through which you and I travel. Joy is birthed by being born anew in Christ, and it cannot be swallowed, bought, achieved, won, or captured. Nonetheless, it is a noble and satisfying fruit, which really has an everlasting quality.

---

1   Philippians 4:12–13.

What does that mean for you and me? It means, friends, God always has the last word. It means that if we are honest enough to bring ourselves to Him, and our needs to Him, whatever those needs may be, He will be honest enough to reveal Himself back to you. It means when you fall into the mud, if you are willing to let Him, God will not leave you wallowing in it. He will help you get up out of whatever mess you find yourself in—if you are just willing to let Him have who you are.

There is a great little playlet by Eugene O'Neil entitled, "Lazarus Laughed." The play takes up in the moments after Jesus raises His friend Lazarus from the grave.[2] It seems that once the bindings fall off of good old Lazarus, he begins at first to giggle, and giggles turns to chuckles, chuckles turns to laughter, and laughter turns to uncontrollable belly laughter! Lazarus, having faced death square in the face, having made it to the other side, having been brought back to life here, is no longer afraid. He knows that if he lets Jesus have all that he is, nothing, not even death can defeat him.

The laughter continues throughout the play, and like most laughter, it is contagious. It begins to turn others to Jesus to the point where his laughter begins to upset the ordered world of the pious Jewish leaders and stoic Roman leaders. When the authorities begin to get upset and threaten Lazarus with imprisonment, he only laughs harder. When they threaten torture, he laughs all the more; finally, the Roman Emperor Tiberius demands his execution, and even then, Lazarus meets death, once again, with laughter. The play ends with the uproarious laughter of Lazarus as he is burned at the stake.

The story, of course, is not to say that pain, suffering, and loss do not matter—but what it does say is that they, when handed over to the transforming power of God, do not ultimately matter; and that is the source for true, authentic joy.

Paul knew that his neck was likely to be greeted with the cold metal of the executioner's axe, and yet he found, even in that—joy, a gift of God that buoys us here, but carries us and greets us in life eternal.

As Lewis wrote, *"Joy is the serious business of heaven."*[3] Indeed. Rejoice in the Lord; and again, I say, rejoice. Amen to that.

---

2   See John 11:1–44.
3   Lewis, *The Joyful Christian*, 228.

Summer Time

To experience joy, one must give way to Jesus Christ. Fearing that anything is beyond His power and control robs us of the freedom that comes from releasing all things—even ourselves—into His loving care. Can you give way to joy?

A PRAYER

Grant to us, O Lord, the royalty of inward happiness, and the serenity which comes from living close to thee. Daily renew in us the sense of joy, and let the eternal Spirit of the Father dwell in our souls and bodies, filling every corner of our hearts with light and grace; so that, bearing about with us the infection of good courage, we may be diffusers of life, and may meet all ills and cross accidents with gallant and high-hearted happiness, giving thee thanks always for all things. Amen.

— Robert Louis Stevenson, d. 1894

Putting Your Gift to Work

"Let no one despise your youth, but set the believers an example in speech and conduct, in love, in faith, in purity. Until I arrive, give attention to the public reading of scripture, to exhorting, to teaching. Do not neglect the gift that is in you, which was given to you through prophecy with the laying on of hands by the council of elders. Put these things into practice, devote yourself to them, so that all may see your progress. Pay close attention to yourself and to your teaching; continue in these things, for in doing this you will save both yourself and your hearers."

— I Timothy 4:12-16

....

Are you using the gift God has given to you?

I have only been snow skiing a few times. The last time, my wife and I were in the Colorado mountains and after a few hours in "ski school" I was ready to put my newly found skills to work. I was horrible—that is perhaps the best word for it.

I could hardly move without fearing for my life, and when I did move, it was usually for short distances and almost always ended with a tumble and fall. I was standing at the peak of one small hill, when not one but several grade school students, some no higher than a few feet tall, scooted around me on all sides with cries of the joy they were experiencing in their own little ski adventure—cries I did not share. Snow skiing is not a gift I possess.

145

As we noted earlier, Paul was a mentor to many, but the one we know the most about is his relationship with Timothy. In the passage above, he gently presses Timothy to carry on in the private and public disciplines of the faith, but he reminds him also not to neglect his particular "gift," which was revealed to him as a prophecy during a time of prayer with others.[1] We are not really sure what Timothy's particular gift was—but Paul urges him not to neglect it and to put it to good use.

I have a friend who used to be captain of the famed *Blue Angels*. This I know for sure—I could never do what he does. I do not have the eyes, the skills, nor the stomach for it. There is a wide gap between this preacher and a fighter pilot, a neurosurgeon, or a concert pianist. That's just the way it is.

Some people look on others' gifts with envy or even despair. That is a foolish choice, as it will lead one to constantly self-evaluate in a way that leads only to one answer—never measuring up, and thus discounting your uniqueness to the world. It may seem rather elementary, but the better choice is not to focus on what is not, but what is. You may be someone who is extraordinarily bright but not so good an athlete, or perhaps a star athlete of average wit. What is your unique, particular gift or set of gifts?

The Anglican priest Nicky Gumbel writes;

> *"Although there is often a family likeness and hopefully, unity in the family, there is also great variety. No two children are identical—not even identical twins are exactly alike. So it is in the body of Christ.*
>
> *"Every Christian is different; each has a different contribution to make, each has a different gift....*
>
> *"All good gifts are from God...."*[2]

---

1   See also I Timothy 1:18 and II Timothy 1:6.
2   Gumbel, *Questions of Life*, 144.

The Bible tells us that as people choose to follow Christ, they are filled with God's Spirit and with that Spirit come particular spiritual gifts and talents.[3] Sometimes these gifts are quite supernatural, such as healing or performing a miracle; and other times they may seem more natural, like hospitality, or teaching. Whatever it is, we should not neglect it nor lag in sharing it.

Paul mentored the Roman Christians to live in such a way that they would be *"living sacrifices"* by pouring out their particular gifts into the lives of others. He tells them,

> *"We have gifts that differ according to the grace given to us: prophecy, in proportion to faith; ministry, in ministering; the teacher, in teaching; the exhorter, in exhortation; the giver, in generosity; the leader, in diligence: the compassionate, in cheerfulness."*[4]

Paul never assumes they would try and trade their gifts in for different ones, as one might trade in a car for a newer one; nor does he entertain that such gifts would not be put to good use. No, the gifts given are especially appointed and they are to be put to good use.

Pastor John Wimber, well known for his teaching on spiritual gifts, writes;

> *"The gifts of the Spirit have nothing to do with personal ambition or career orientation. They are not given to build individual reputations, to warrant superior positions in the local church, or to demonstrate spiritual advancement. They are not trophies, but tools—tools for touching and blessing others."*[5]

As summer gives way to autumn, consider not just the particular gifts you have, but ways that you can use them to more fully bless the lives of others, for like every good gift, it is always better when it is shared.

---

3   See Romans 12:3–8 and I Corinthians 12.
4   Romans 12:1, 6–8.
5   John Wimber, "Spiritual Gifts," in *The Westminster Collection of Christian Quotations*, 356.

Summer Time

Write here a list of your particular gifts. It might be helpful to write a list of gifts you do not have as well! That way, you can begin to rid yourself of envy and turn instead to gratitude; and in doing so taking Paul's words to Timothy as your own, *"Do not neglect the gift that is within you...put these things into practice."*

A Prayer

O Lord, without Whom our labour is but lost, and with Whom the weakest go forth as the mighty; be present to all works in Thy Church which are undertaken according to Thy will, and grant to thy labourers a pure intention, patient faith, sufficient success upon earth, and the bliss of serving Thee in heaven; through Jesus Christ our Lord. Amen.

— William Bright, d. 1901

The Safest of All Places

"God is love, and those who abide in love abide in God, and God abides in them. Love has been perfected among us in this: that we may have boldness on the day of judgment, because as he is, so are we in this world. There is no fear in love, but perfect love casts out fear..."

— I John 4:16b-18a

Our journey of shared time has come to an end, but each day brings a few opportunities to allow summer time to breathe afresh in and through us and carry us safely, along with those we know and love, to the vesper light.

Having served the church for virtually my entire adult life, I have found that perhaps more than anything people want to know they are loved. In a personal way, of course, we all want love from friends, family, and others closest to us. But it seems because human love is often fraught with frailty and imperfection, we hunger for a perfect love. We have that, already, in God.

When we are children, we are comforted by simple verses like *"Jesus loves the little children, all the children of the world"* and *"He's got the whole world in His hands."* But as we grow older, our simple faith is often challenged, by our own failings and those of others; by the scars and wounds of life, by angst and worry; all of which are born in some kind of fear that God will abandon us, leave us, stop loving us. But God cannot stop loving, for He Himself *is* love.

God's love in Christ forgives and redeems, reassures and restores. It heals and makes whole. It, in every way that can be imagined, saves us.

It is our hope that *Summer Times* has been a reminder of God's love for you—that you are always within His circle of care. I opened this little work taking note of the many journeys we shared with my grandmother, Grantzy. Let me close with one more.

One of the places we often visited with Grantzy was an old log cabin. Grantz told us it was built by one of my great grandfathers. It had several rooms, large stone fireplaces, and a trap door to the root cellar where she told us slaves stayed as they tried to make their way north to safety. (I need to add that Grantz had a tendency to tell tall tales from time to time!)

There was a large barn set across from the front door of the cabin and a smokehouse once used for curing meat. There was no electricity, no heat, or air conditioning. There was no running water—so there was an outhouse (which I think every child should have to experience!) and a spring nearby where, when taking up temporary residence in the cabin, we would bathe—downstream from where we pulled out our drinking water with large plastic milk jugs Grantz brought along.

We decided to name the place "Happy Holler," because that was a place that felt safe, and was full of adventure, good memories and good times.

150

One visit was different though. We arrived late in the day, and the house had been ransacked. Pieces of the fireplace had been knocked loose; there was broken glass everywhere. The modest furniture that had been there was either stolen or broken apart. Someone had invaded our safe little world. We just wanted to turn and leave.

But it was too late, and Grantz' pioneer spirit prevailed. Before long, she had made a makeshift fire, supper was underway, and my sisters and I were munching on sugar cane on the back porch. When it came time for bed, Grantz plopped down an old bedspring she found. She covered it with sheets and blankets and there my sisters and I slept, with her nearest the door.

Sometime in the middle of the night I woke up. My grandmother was missing and a loud screech owl began yelling from the barn.

I first heard something in the room with us, and then saw a large dark figure move between the door and us kids. I whispered out, "Grantz? Is that you?"

She whispered back, "Yes dear..." "What are you doing?" I asked. "I am marking a circle of kerosene around the bed to keep the snakes and bugs away. It's okay...everything is okay...you are safe here...go back to sleep." She continued to draw her little circle of protection that guarded us through that night. I could rest in that.

A postscript here...When I grew up and had kids of my own, I spent a day going back to "Happy Holler." I took two of my kids. It was very hard to find. In fact, while finding it I realized that it had not been built by one of my ancestors, and when Grantz would take us there, we were likely trespassing on private property every time!

But with my kids in tow, we trespassed again. We walked the long trail and found that cabin in the woods, which, through my adult eyes, now seemed so small. The smoke house was gone; so was the outhouse. We went inside and snooped around a bit...there was the trap door...the back porch where we ate sugar cane.

As we moved into that main front room, there, propped up against a wall, was an old rusty bed spring—the same one that years and years before we took rest upon in a place that had been invaded by what, or children, seemed like a dark force. It was almost like a symbol, a sacrament of sorts... an outward and visible sign of the mystery of God's safe haven.

Then I remembered my grandmother and her whisper in the dark—"It's okay...I am just drawing a little circle of protection around us.... everything is okay...you are safe here."

We call the light that surrounds us at day's end the vesper light. The word *vesper* finds its origin in Latin and Greek, and it marks the beginning of evening. Since the earliest days of the church, vesper services usually began around 6:00 p.m., or sundown, when the light of this world began to dim, candles were lit to show the way, and incense burned to accompany worship.

We need not fear the vesper light, or the coming of darkness, or summer's end. God is always, always watching over us. While there are things we can do and choices we can make that resist God's love for us; while we can even reject His love, He never stops loving. Never.

God is constantly seeking to draw us into His love. As we receive Him into our lives, we will come to know His love and that love will serve as solace to our fears and worries. As we come to trust it more and more, we will rest increasingly secure.

Be not afraid of the vesper light—whenever or wherever it greets you. God is in the midst of it, lighting the way to His peace, His life, His love—the safest of all places.

A PRAYER

Father of the human race,
Jesus who redeems the same;
Send forth Thy Spirit to lead the way;
To forgive when I have sinned,
To heal when I am broken,
To lift when I am low,
To comfort when I do grieve.

And when all is well,
To give me gladness,
To grant me gratitude,
To make me generous.

Where I lack,
O Trinity of God,
Fill me;
And where I am too full,
Empty me,
That I may be to others,
And to Thee,
What Thou dost desire;

Be there O God,
At my waking,
With my working,
In my sleeping;

And journey with me, I pray,
To Thine perfect end
And then onward and into
Thy perfect Kingdom and
Thy everlasting rest.
Amen.

Scripture Index

155

Author Index